# FOR THOSE TEARS I DIED

The Intriguing Story of a Song's Message
That Brought Healing to Millions and Helped
Birth Contemporary Christian Music

By

## Marsha Stevens-Pino

© 2016

For Those Tears I Died
The Intriguing Story of a Song's Message That Brought Healing to
Millions and Helped Birth Contemporary Christian Music

Author: Marsha Stevens-Pino

Published by: Canyonwalker Press
Reno, NV USA
www.CanyonWalkerPress.com

Cover design by: Carolyn Woodard
Developmental Editor: Jerry Reiter
Copy Editor: Elaine Bellamore Phillips
Photography: Mark Moseley

Most Scriptures quoted are from the HOLY BIBLE, NEW
INTERNATIONAL VERSION [NIV] Copyright © 1973, 1978,
1984, 1990, 2011 International Bible Society. Zondervan Bible
Publishers.

Library of Congress Control Number: 2016952193

ISBN: 978-1619200555

# DEDICATION

To my patient Savior and to the wife who always reminds me to be more like Him.

# Acknowledgements

Writing this book has been far more of an experience than I ever expected. I started out writing it with the help and support of Dr. James Brix (Doctor of Ministry in Marriage and Family from Palmer Theological Seminary in Philadelphia). Jim is a good friend and an even better voice of encouragement. When Jim and I hit a wall in the organizational content of the book, friend and author, Darlene Bogle stepped in to take a thousand thoughts and hammer them into one story. I still can't believe she did it. They both continue to be invaluable parts of my life and ministry - and two of my biggest cheerleaders.

Several people came together to support my writing time. Some of them have asked not to be mentioned by name, but I have to thank Sherry Lynne Stargel for funding tremendous support for several weeks of writing. My fellow songwriters have helped me to tell the truths I could never express any other way. Like anyone blessed with many friends, I dread leaving someone out. I hope you all know that you make me who I am and you make my ministry possible. Please take ownership in that.

My kids and family are my everyday world and I trust they feel the love I have for each of them, but Cindy is my rock. Somehow we have come to run this three-legged race of life together and my story would not have the passion or joy it does without her. When we first started dating we decided we would be like the airlines and have a "two pieces of baggage" rule about what we brought to the relationship. We both have exceeded that at times, or ended up shifting weight from one suitcase to the other, but we have managed to stay aloft and she strengthens me in ways I could never explain.

# Table of Contents

# FOREWORD BY PEGGY CAMPOLO

When I finished reading this book, I knew I had read *two* stories. The one I had expected to read was the inspiring life story of a dear friend who has held fast to her Lord ever since, as a broken and needy child, she met Jesus. Marsha Stevens-Pino has trusted God through more pain, rejection and disappointment than most of us will ever know.

The surprise, or the book-within-a-book, is the one about the history of The Jesus Movement of the 1960's and 70's. Marsha, as a member of the band, Children of the Day, was part of that history, and the men and women who were an integral part of The Jesus Movement come to life as their stories are woven into her own. Marsha worked with some of the biggest names in Jesus Music, who would become today's worldwide Contemporary Christian Music (CCM) artists.

Andrae Crouch (Soon and Very Soon), Love Song (Little Country Church), Second Chapter of Acts (Easter Song), Matthew Ward (Toward Eternity - Noah's Song). There are some surprising interactions with Pat Boone and Kris Kristofferson, too.

Marsha's interactions with them all are told with forthright honesty, but always in the light of the love she felt for them. Men and women who had been only names to me became real people as I saw them minister in the name of Jesus, worship, make mistakes, fail and succeed brilliantly through her eyes.

You may have sung "For Those Tears I Died (Come to the Water)," the hymn Marsha wrote when, at the age of 16, she first knew that Jesus loved her, but you cannot understand the depths of pain from which that song came until you know the beginning and the middle of the story of the woman who wrote it. She was a lesbian who fell in love with Jesus, only to have the earthly church of Jesus Christ tell her she and her gifts were unacceptable to them or to Jesus because of who she was. But, the main thing is that Marsha never heard Jesus tell her that. She makes it clear that it is only because she came to understand that Jesus loved her unconditionally that her story did not end badly. Indeed, Marsha's story has not ended at all. She has become a heroic figure who refuses to embrace a false identity to be accepted by those in the church she loves.

In so many ways, Marsha has forged for others a path to Jesus. She and her life partner Cindy Stevens-Pino work tirelessly and sacrificially to keep their company, BALM (Born Again Lesbian Music) actively engaged in its ministry which includes her concerts, recordings, and a newsletter that not only brings hope to those children of God who happen not to be straight, but informs in fresh and new ways those of us who are straight. BALM's newest ministry is finding, training and encouraging young artists who, like Marsha, have good reason to wonder if their musical gifts can be used by God.

Marsha uses her God-given gifts of music, beauty, and charisma to let her audiences know that Jesus Christ is the real foundation of her life. The first time I saw her minister, it was to an audience of tired and weary people who knew too well the rejection of much of the church. As Marsha sang and talked to them, that audience came alive. It was as though she had watered flowers just as they were about to die of thirst. Truly, she had brought to those people the living water.

When you finish this book, you will feel as blessed to know Marsha Stevens-Pino as I do.

Peggy Campolo

# Prologue

January 2016, Houston TX

The Hilton shuttle picked us up at the airport and we started talking before we even got to the hotel. "Are you going to the Gay Christian Network (GCN) Conference?" Eight out of ten of us chimed in, "YES!"

One twenty-something woman in the back was coming as a reporter for *Sojourners*, a Disciples of Christ denominational magazine. The rest of us introduced ourselves too, but when it got to me (the oldest person on the shuttle!) I said my name and the reporter said, "Wait! I think you're in the encyclopedia that we keep in our break room." So the conference officially began as she pulled out her iPad and made the first note.

She would go on to report, after we arrived at the Hilton, that there were 1,500 "racially diverse, variously-aged attendees from 48 states, 17 countries and just about every denomination from Mennonite to Seventh-Day Adventist (with particularly strong representation from conservative evangelical and nondenominational churches.) Attendees included Christians who identified as gay, lesbian, bisexual, transgender, intersex, asexual, and queer, as well as straight allies, parents of LGBTQ people, and those still exploring their own identities."

I was checked into the hotel by cheery staff who assured me that they were happy to host this event - especially since the city of Houston had only recently revoked its anti-discrimination ordinance against LGBTQ people, and the Hilton wanted to be sure we knew that they did, in fact, support the LGBTQ community.

I saw old friends who, as is often the case, immediately wanted me to meet their parents or their pastors. Even all these years after I came out, so many of them see me as a bridge-builder from my generation of committed "Jesus People" Christians to younger believers and seekers in the LGBTQ community.

I'm happy to share experiences, Scripture, music; whatever helps us see one another's hearts. Then I saw Hannah and Dar - women from my home church, Pass-a-grille Community (PAG) in St. Pete, Florida. With her characteristic exuberance my friend Hannah flew across the room to greet me.

I first met Hannah in 2014 when our pastor told me there were some women he wanted me to meet. Generally this was a bit of code for, "I'm not sure they know they will be welcomed here; will you make sure they are?" I had walked into the same service 4 years earlier wondering that same thing.

Even as I walked up, I could see that they were "family" to each other and to me; two women who loved Jesus and also loved each other. Dar was tall and quiet, but Hannah was a spitfire; 20 years old, tiny with pixie blonde hair and intense blue eyes. And she wanted to know right away who I was. She softened as I explained just a sentence or two of my background, my music, one of my songs that even her fundamentalist mother loved...and then she was full of questions.

As her story spilled out, I was torn between reassurance and horror. Reassurance that they had found a home and that we would love them here and help them grow in Christ. Horror that 34 years after I had been rejected by Calvary Chapel Costa Mesa, she had been asked to leave Calvary Chapel in Saint Petersburg. I could hear Jesus pleading with His disciples in Mark, "Having eyes, see ye not? And having ears, hear ye not?"

How was it possible that people had looked at the energetic, eager, child-woman and told her she was not welcome in church? That she was going to hell? How could her mother post online that she would rather her daughter have a millstone put around her neck *and be cast out to drown rather than be gay?*

*So at the GCN conference, between classes, seminars, concerts and testimonies, Hannah and her partner set aside time for me to share with them in the hotel room. And I sat down to tell her stories about my tears, my Savior, and the songs I love to share.*

# 1
# FAMILY SECRETS

Like most people, I only learned about my parents' past after I was older. Adults often say that children should come with an Instruction Manual. I always thought that parents should come with one.

I knew that during the years of World War II, Daddy had been a pastor. He had, in fact, pastored a couple of churches. I was told fuzzy reasons for why he was no longer a pastor. "Doctrinal differences" or "church politics," were two of the usual excuses.

It was not until I was in my 20's that I learned that Daddy, Pastor Edwin, had been driven out of several churches, and at least one church at gunpoint, by the fathers of young girls he had molested. One of the young church-goers my father molested was Winna. I knew her name because she became my mother.

When Winna was 13, she met Pastor Edwin, who was 35 and already married with two small children. She was a prodigy on the violin and a talented singer. He put her in charge of the junior choir and ultimately the main choir. My future Daddy was the handsome darling of the church, outgoing and energetic and always had something going for the "young people."

One night he dropped Winna off last from the youth activities of the evening. Winna was excited that Pastor Edwin paid so much attention to her. She thought she was his favorite. But that night his "attention" became obsession and then rape.

Winna ended the night devastated and disillusioned about his caring for her. He told her that he wouldn't tell anyone that they had "fallen in love", but she had to keep it a secret, too; that if she told anyone his little son and daughter would lose their Daddy and, worst of all,

Winna's own mother would have a stroke and die. After all, she had problems with her blood pressure. Having a man of God say this with such certainty made it seem believable.

Winna's own family situation growing up was -- puzzling. She was told her father died in a fire when she was 2 years old. They said he had gotten drunk with some friends in an abandoned house, passed out and someone had knocked over a candle or lamp and caused a fire. This was not true, but Winna did not know it, yet.

She had a family member named Pete, who stayed in her Mom's home from time to time and helped to raise her, but since they were not married, they called him a "cousin". Most of her immediate family members were Oklahoma Cherokees who had fled the reservation and did all they could to avoid discussion about it. Her "cousin's" real name was King Diamond Star but, for reasons I didn't understand, there was shame about coming from a reservation. They did leave the reservation just before the time my mother was born. King Diamond Star changed his name to Pete. In later years he told Winna and his other children that he was her father. "Cousin Pete" was really Dad.

Pete was not often around and Winna lived alone with her mother, Jesse. She and her mother were very close. Edwin saw that which is why he came up with the 'prophecy' that her mother would have a stroke and die if she told her about their 'love affair." This was terrifying to her, especially since Edwin convinced Winna their sexual relationship was due to her coming on to him (a common tactic of those who abuse children).

Such a big secret required a string of lies. Pastor Edwin's machinations of pubescent Winna were a travesty. He made her practice lying. He told her to steal something from his secretary's desk. Then he would tell Winna to tell the secretary she had not stolen anything. Or he would have Winna stand next to him behind his desk, and make her smile convincingly to a parishioner while he surreptitiously reached up under her dress out of the church member's sight.

He made her promise to burn all the notes and letters he sent her. He sent them to a post office box and told her where to go to read and then destroy them. He convinced her that she was the one who had actually seduced him so that even many decades later, shortly after my Dad died, Mom would tell me, "As you've probably guessed by now, your father and I had an affair before we were married." She had internalized the blame and concluded that even at 13 it was all her fault.

Edwin controlled her life throughout high school. One time Pete found a note that Winna had failed to destroy and he confronted Edwin about it. My father was adept at lying and misdirection. He managed to convince Pete it was some sort of exercise he was doing with the youth group. To keep from upsetting Winna's mother, Pete backed off. And given his own secrets, Pete was not the one to throw the first stone.

Shortly after that incident, Edwin was instrumental in getting Winna a full music scholarship to Redlands University in California. He "visited" her there every Saturday and she was expected to keep the day free for him. Somehow she managed to compartmentalize Saturdays from the rest of her life. She met a boy she liked and began getting to know him.

One Friday night Edwin came up early and saw her holding hands with the boy. He immediately went to the dean as Winna's "concerned pastor" and suggested that Winna was "too close" to someone on campus, implying that she was behaving inappropriately with the boy. He got her transferred to Chapman College before the next semester began, her scholarship intact, but her fate sealed.

When my mother finally graduated from college and got her teaching credential, she felt she could try one more time to tell her mother what had been going on for over eight years and see if she could break free. When she did, her mother actually did have a stroke and die, fulfilling Edwin's prophecy. Edwin then divorced his first wife and married my mother. Years later she would tell me, "I will always believe I killed my mother."

Winna threw herself into starting a family, pleasing her new husband, and charming his son and daughter from his first marriage; they lived with their own mother but visited. Winna had a distressing miscarriage before having me and one again before having my sister Wendy. People always described my mother as "overprotective" and I think she sort of liked that characterization. We waited precisely one hour after any eating to swim, even in the small backyard play pool. We had doctor check-ups and dentist visits every 6 months without fail. We were never allowed to play in the street. She gave away the family cocker spaniel/mix after it accidentally knocked me down when I was two years old.

Mom was a schoolteacher, usually a substitute, so she was home when we were home. The problem, of course, was that even with her best efforts she couldn't protect me in the way I would most need protection. My mother's best efforts to keep us safe from the world were ineffective when it came to my father's physical, verbal and sexual abuse.

I was born on August 20th, 1952 and from my earliest memory, my mother slept in one room with me, and my father slept in the other bedroom. Even after my sister was born, "the girls" slept in a room together and Daddy had his own room. Fear and love were intertwined in ugly ways during my childhood.

Alcohol had been the bane of our existence. My father always had liquor at night, beer during the day. It was the grown up drink and it seemed perfectly normal at first. It went along with his cherry-wood pipe smoke to make up the scent of our childhood evenings. I was never certain quite when alcohol became the overwhelming fact of our lives. But it did.

Daddy was an angry man. It seemed to hover just behind his eyes. Drop a tool, forget to do a chore, spill the milk, fail to find an item he sent you to fetch, and his eyes turned to those of a rabid wolf. As a very young child I identified him in the horrible wolves of fairy tales.

I remember telling my mother a recurring nightmare I had when I was 5 or 6. I was sitting on my mother's lap in the living room of our home when a wolf ran through the door. My mother abruptly stood up, dumped me onto the floor and left the room. I was terrified. The wolf attacked me and then left. As soon as the wolf left, my mother came back into the room and gathered me up into her arms, cooing at me. She put Band-Aids on all my wounds. Then the wolf came back and she threw me off her lap and left the room as she had before, allowing the wolf to assault me again.

My mother assured me I had just heard too many fairy tales and she was not going to read *Little Red Riding Hood or The Three Little Pigs* to me ever again. This didn't solve the problem, or prevent the nightmares.

Later, when my parents told me about having a baby sister, they somehow failed to convey to me that this was their other daughter. The only thing they told me is that they were bringing me home a baby sister. It was 1955 when Wendy was born and became my little sister. That's how they referred to her anytime that I was around, and that's precisely how I thought of her. She was mine. Just as if they had brought me home a goldfish or a kitten, it would be my responsibility, right? I doted on her, helped dress and feed her. I was thrilled from the moment I saw her. Charles and Kay, my half-brother and half-sister, named her Wendy from their favorite book, *Peter Pan*.

In first grade, when I was six and Wendy was three, our class was told to draw a picture of our families. I dutifully drew mine and labeled them for the teacher by name. Mrs. Taylor said, "Oh, so you have a mommy and a daddy and two daughters." I protested that I had no such thing. We had a mommy and a daddy and a daughter and a baby sister. I argued so heatedly with her that she reported the incident to my mother. I was aghast. Wendy was not their other daughter. She was mine – my baby sister. How could they change that?

In practice, nothing actually did change that much. I continued to be Wendy's protector whenever I could. When my father's wrath came down, I tried to be as brave as I could to take the "spankings" (which were so much worse than that). If I could at least get him to start with me, I thought his rage might cool by the time he got to her. More than once his promise that he would "spank us till we couldn't sit down" came true. I remember drawing my sister's bath and having to gently lay her down in the tub. The bruises covering Wendy, from mid-back to her knees, were too swollen for her to bend in order to sit down. I helped her stand and dry and put her to bed ... and seethed. I saw that my mother's occasional protests only earned her outright beatings. It seemed to me that my father drank more after beating us, which only led to all night dramas where he raged and ranted at all of us for making him angry.

I pulled my sister away from Disney's "Wonderful World of Color" on the television set my half-brother Charles had built himself from a Heath Kit. He had told us to be careful with the vacuum tubes inside the back of the TV "because they can explode." I know now that he meant you could get a shard of glass in your finger because of breaking the vacuum if we dropped a tube. But my sister and I pictured a small bomb going off, so I was always very careful when she was around it. Once my father was too drunk to realize he had tipped the TV on top of Wendy and she lay underneath it until I got home to lift it off.

We had moved to an old four-bedroom, two story house when I was 8, so each of us had our own room. Mine was at the very head of the stairs, with my father's on one side and my mother's on the other. Wendy's was protectively at the far end of the hall, with her own half bath.

I always tried to get Wendy safely into her bed at the end of the hall away from my father's room before I climbed into bed myself. It was an older house with creaky floors, so I would hear anyone who was sneaking down the hall. I was never allowed to have a door on my bedroom. I was not sure why that was, but it was a given fact of life.

The open door into my room was at the head of the stairs. Many nights would start quietly. Then I would hear my father's steps on the stairs. Sure enough, it was only moments before the shouting started. My father was bellowing about why my mother was still walking around, why she smelled of alcohol, why she was watching the television in his room.

My mother's words were slurred and she couldn't make sense. This would start my father's search for her stash of pills or booze, with banging cupboards and slamming drawers. My mother hung onto his ankles to slow him down. I could hear her being dragged from room to room, begging him to stop. Occasionally I would hear the thud of him kicking her free of him. Then a scream as he picked her up by her hair and threw her in her own bed and slammed the door.

Quiet ensued and I went back to sleep. I was awakened again by slow creaking floors and I was instantly at my door to see if anyone was creeping down the hall to my sister's room, but it was my mother trying to sneak down the stairs for more of whatever she was taking or drinking to quiet her demons. My heart sank. If I heard her, so did he. But tonight he waited until she was down there to confront her. That meant another hour's sleep before the screaming, shouting and breaking of bottles in the sink began. My father would check each of his own bottles to see if they seemed watered down or depleted.

They were away from my sister, so I went back to sleep. The ruckus continued upstairs as he dragged my mother, by this time completely incoherent and compliant, and threw her into her bed with a curse. Once again I pulled my head under the covers. I hated it under there. It was hot and made me feel smothered, but I was comforted by the idea that perhaps I would suffocate. When you grow up with alcoholics in the house, you learn that night is the time to hide. "To sleep, perchance to dream" …perhaps to die. Wouldn't that be a relief? I didn't know anything about heaven, but anywhere had to be better than here.

Although I didn't know the terms "hebephilia" (a sexual preference for children in early pubescence), or "ephebophilia" (sexual preference for adolescents) until adulthood, they were part of my childhood reality. I experienced them personally. I thought of it at first as my "very bad spankings," and all I really knew about them was that they made me bleed when I went to the bathroom. I had no understanding of sexual pleasure. My father simply seemed angry to me.

All I actually remember about the first injury was waking up from a bad dream and starting for my mother's bed when I remembered she was sick, so I went to my father's room instead. Sometime later that night, I was standing in the hallway thinking, "*Stupid stupid stupid. I am so dumb. I know better than to wake him up at night.*"

My mother wanted to take me to the doctor, my father railed against that, but the bleeding got so bad they took me to surgery to repair rectal fissures. I was in the hospital for a week. No doctor or social worker ever spoke to me about how I had sustained this damage, nor did it occur to me that this was something I needed to disclose. I only knew that these things happened when no one else was around. This made me have an even more vigilant and wary eye upon my father to keep him from being alone with my sister.

While the surgery put him off for a while, my father ultimately renewed his interest by wanting to teach me "sex education" in explicit step-by-step details. I squirmed and plotted, doing anything I could to be sure I was between him and my sister and preferably that both of us were somewhere else entirely. The ploys ultimately worked in Wendy's case, but not for others. I was not relieved of his attentions nor, it turned out, were many of my friends, neighbors and relatives.

Even in my 40s and 50s as social networks connected me to people from my past I heard from more of my childhood friends about my father's molestations. But at least my sister was spared. I think it was actually a relief for my father, as well. There was one person he hadn't violated in that way and he felt he was his best self around her. It allowed them to have a relationship I could never enjoy.

When he felt his best, he was expansive and engaging. He told tales and quoted poems and orated "The Cremation of Sam McGee" for all who would listen. He told the same jokes over and over and engaged my friends in games of fortune telling or personality quizzes like those you see today online – "answer this series of questions and I'll tell you who you really are inside." In the community, he worked for the LA Board of Supervisors and LA County, both as a probation officer and in other city capacities. He was vehement for civil rights, even as early on as protesting the internment of Japanese US citizens in World War II.

Daddy owned lemon groves in San Dimas. He hired itinerant workers to tend the trees and harvest, and working with them kept him occupied and out of the house for long hours. I was always to address the workers in the same way I did other adults, respectfully and in their own language. "Buenos dias, Señor Gutierrez, cómo está usted?"(Good day, Mr. Gutierrez, how are you?) A side benefit was that I learned some Spanish. But it was also a lesson in human and racial equality.

We were not allowed to watch the Little Rascals because my parents felt they mistreated Buckwheat; same for Amos 'n' Andy because it depicted African-Americans as unintelligent. While my father's concern for ethnic groups was admirable, and I am very grateful for the way I was raised in that regard, his treatment of his own family was lacking in integrity.

My mother tried to pre-empt my father's punishments by doing her own spankings and assuring him they had been done. She taught me to stand by the window with the curtain opened as my father pulled in the driveway each night and instructed me to jump up and down and clap my hands. As early as 3 years old, I learned to carefully empty his ashtray and bring him his grown up drink. And, of course, I learned to sing. Performances were prepared at least weekly for my father, but I also had charming songs to learn for visitors from his work and for my grandfather and other family guests.

'Grampa Ray' was my father's dad and the only living person I ever called a grandparent. Daddy's mother had died before I was born. My favorite thing about Grampa was his poetry. It seemed as though he knew every poem ever written. On Wednesday nights we would visit and he would regale us with stories from Ali Baba and the 40 Thieves, quote Scheherazade or the poem of Abou Ben Adhem. He knew all of Shakespeare's sonnets and hundreds of poems by Wordsworth, Longfellow and Keats. It was honestly the best of my education. I learned that "only God can make a tree" (Trees by Joyce Kilmer), that God can hear anyone's plea (The Fool's Prayer by Edward Sill), that we each speak in our own language (Each in His Own Tongue by William Carruth), and what the apostle Peter went through when he was martyred (Domine, Quo Vadis? by William Watson).

My favorite story from Grampa Ray's own childhood had to do with his memorizations. It seemed that his class was assigned the task of memorizing at least a few lines of Longfellow's The Song of Hiawatha to recite in class (the poem is over 100 pages long). The next week Grampa Ray walked (you know, barefoot and uphill both ways, but at least he was in California!) to school, which started at 7:00 AM. Since his last name was "Carter" and they went alphabetically, he was the first. He began to recite his memorized verses just after school started and he continued until they had to stop him 5 hours later to break for lunch.

I so loved poetry and the way that it touched my heart that I began to memorize, too. I was never like Grampa, but as soon as I'd master one, I'd be all over quoting to anyone who would sit still long enough to listen. I got my sister Wendy into it when she was old enough to learn four lines at a time and this was her first:

*"He drew a circle that shut me out-*
*Heretic, rebel - a thing to flout.*
*But love and I had the wit to win:*
*We drew a circle and took him in!"* (Edwin Markham)

It would be many years before either of us knew what a "heretic" was, but when I found out, this little poem was awfully good information.

Elementary school through the 3rd grade was mostly about keeping me busy. Other than my near-catastrophic revelation about Wendy being my parents' other daughter, my early school days centered on keeping my best friend, Susan, and me out of trouble. There were three classes for each grade and they were clearly marked as upper, middle and lower learning levels. Susan and I tested as "upper" in academics, but clearly not in behavior. The school experimented with separating us, but being bored only made us more troublesome. We did go to church and Sunday school together. Very little of it was personal to either of us.

The flannel board characters of Old Testament stories were told with the same attentiveness as a fairy-tale. We knew "David and Goliath" the same way we knew "Cinderella," and I don't think we would have thought anyone believed either story was true. The main event was getting treats in the fellowship hall or going out for doughnuts together with our families, and that's really how I thought of church. Monday through Friday one attended school. Sunday mornings one attended church before getting doughnuts.

When we moved to the house in Claremont the elementary school had a music class with an excellent teacher. The 4th grade through 6th grade choir there did three-part harmonies and Miss Corbeil was very strict about behavior. It took me half of 4th grade to get my behavior under control enough that she let me into choir. It was my first experience being thought of as a singer outside of my family, and it was something I loved to do. It proved to be something that kept me out of a lot of trouble for the rest of school – at least it was a deterrent to worse behavior.

I also had my very first crush in 4th grade. It was nobody in class; it was a crush on my teacher, Mrs. Seed. I would be one of the last students to leave every day, so that I could kiss her cheek good-bye. I kept a diary back then that I still have. In it I wrote that I told Mrs. Seed I had one wish on the last day of school. I was going to ask her for a four-letter word that starts with "K". Mrs. Seed understood my request and on the last day of school I wrote that she did kiss my cheek. I wrote that I wasn't going to wash it for a week. What was I then, a 10-year-old kid?

School was my refuge from home and family. Even simple things turned ugly. Camping trips, for instance, a staple in our family, inevitably became agony. Backing the car in or, God forbid, a camper trailer, became a shouting-match over who said to turn which way and how.

This was followed by getting out the level-tool to make sure the bubble was right in the middle in all directions so that the camper was perfectly level. Tents had to be set up properly, tent pegs nailed into the right depth, no stones under the tarp. All of this was accomplished with much lashing of tongues - and belts - before we were done.

Once or twice my half-brother, Charles, came to give the girls (my mother, sister and me) a break. He would do all the set-up, take my father's shouting and cursing with a grin and a wink for us and make it seem easy. One time my father told him to set the parking brake on the car. He did, but when he stepped out of the car, it rolled forward perhaps 6 inches before settling. My father screamed at him, "When I say 'pull that brake' I mean PULL it!"

My brother calmly reached into the car, planted his foot on the doorframe and pulled the parking brake right out of the car. I was amazed and delighted. He was my hero for standing up to our father.

Dad's next step, I noticed, was to bring out the beer. By then my father was drinking copious amounts of alcohol in the evenings or on camping trips, and generally it calmed him down. He still did things that were sexually inappropriate or inconsiderate, but it cut down on his anger.

That night Charles and Wendy and I slept outside in our sleeping bags while my mother and father slept in the camper. Charles woke us up to watch him prank our father. First he hit something over on the metal trash bins and people who stayed up all night to see a bear all turned their flashlights on at once.

Charles, in only his underwear and a t-shirt, ran quickly out of their light beams and over to our camper where he made low growling bear sounds under the window and rocked the camper slightly. Then he ran to us and jumped back into his sleeping bag. He showed us how to put our hands near our faces and bite on a finger to keep from giggling so we could watch as our father came out to look for the bear. Dad shouted out to shoo the bear away and walked around in circles looking for the bear.

It made the sight even funnier since we were trying not to be heard laughing. But we laughed long after Dad had given up and gone back to bed. We were still laughing the next morning as our dad told other campers the story of how he chased a bear out of camp last night. The camping excursions were fun, and I continued those kinds of trips when I had my own children. They were happier and more carefree days, especially if my brother came along. But when Charles was off to grad school at MIT and to get his PhD at Rockefeller, things became scarier again.

My father's anger and abuse increased when there was no one to stop him. At some point my mother decided it was time to stand up to my father. I remember the first time being shocked that she confronted him on anything. We were in the car. He pulled to the side of the road and pushed her out on the curb. Only once or twice more that I saw personally did she make the attempt to oppose my dad, and each time she was overpowered by his aggression. Gradually I began to notice that she was drinking with him in the evening.

If anyone has ever wondered about alcoholism being a "disease," my mother would have convinced you of the dramatically different physical effects it has on some people. I'm serious when I say that half of a beer would turn her into a different person. Even in retrospect it's frightening. As a child it was terrifying.

It was as though my mother sat down on the sofa and a beast arose. She would make a hideous face; curl her hands into claws, or growl and moan. This was a schoolteacher, a choir director, a violinist, a cook and homemaker. She was gentle, helpful, uncomplaining. She included people who were left out, remembered names and places, facts and friends. She stayed up all night to nurse baby kittens, planned birthday parties, and carried everyone's towels out to the beach. But once she picked up the first drink, she became someone else.

One of the blessings and horrors of my childhood was adaptability. My sister and I adapted to my mother's drinking. Arguing over whose turn it was to take care of her became like an argument over whose turn it was to do the dishes.

I have a seared memory of my sister and me standing on either side of my mother's unconscious body lying on the floor. We had cleaned her up, but she clearly needed more help and we were arguing over whose turn it was to take her to the emergency room. She mixed pills with the alcohol and sometimes had prescriptions in different variations of her name. She would use her maiden name or her middle name and that would appear on her prescription bottles. I know because we tried to gather them up every time we took her to the emergency room.

For many years, we kept that secret in the family. The day finally came when she drank at work in her kindergarten class. The principal called mystified. He said someone had to come and get Mrs. Carter, because she was crouched in a corner of the kindergartner's coat closet and no one could coax her out. We were mortified by her behavior, of course. But her own humiliation was so all-consuming to her that ours paled in comparison. Embarrassment was sometimes the least of the problems we would face.

# 2
# IF YOU LOVE ME, SAVE MY LIFE

At the age of 12, I became very ill. My mother took me to a physician at our HMO who said I had the stomach flu. I got sicker and complained of terrible pain in my abdomen. My mother called the doctor who reiterated his opinion and said that kids sometimes just try to get attention and I only had the flu. I started vomiting. My fever went up.

My father came into the room screaming at me that I was just being a baby and that I would 'never grow up and be a woman if I couldn't handle a little stomach pain.' The 'be a woman' line had come up frequently and I was never sure if it was a euphemism for having a baby or some other pain he thought women should be able to endure.

Ultimately my fever topped 104. I was unable to stand up straight. I looked into my mother's eyes and for the ONLY time in my life said, "If you love me, take me to the hospital."
She looked at my angry father and got me an aspirin instead. In that moment, whatever tiny bit of a handle I thought I had on my own destiny burned away with my fever. I knew right then that I had no power in this world; not to protect myself or my sister, not even to save my own life.

By morning I was delirious. She took me back to the HMO doctor who sent me straight to the hospital. When she finally got me to the emergency room it seemed to me as though everything went into fast forward. People bustled all over me, drawing blood, starting IV's and prepping for surgery. But I was only dimly aware that someone believed me that something was wrong with me and they were going to try to fix it.

I heard the ER doc on the other side of the curtain. "So, mother of the year, where have you been for the past four days?" It was a terrible thing to say to my over-protective Mom and, of course, she decided to kill the pain with alcohol.

I had apparently started out with appendicitis. But after it had been misdiagnosed and ignored for several days, my appendix had ruptured, spreading infection first throughout my abdomen and female organs and finally into my bloodstream. I was septic (filled with putrid bacteria) with inflammation caused by peritonitis (damage to the thin lining of the abdomen) before they finally brought me to the ER.

The surgeons opened my abdomen, removed damaged tissue, flushed out all the infection they could and matter-of-factly told me I would probably not be able to have children. Wow, way to drop a bomb on a kid. They left several drains in me for a week or so. I had a tube down my nose to keep my stomach decompressed, a catheter into my bladder and IV lines to flood my bloodstream with antibiotics.

They let my father into Critical Care to see me and I managed to speak around the tubes, "Who's a baby now?" It was the only time I remember actually thinking that I hurt my father because he looked overcome. I could only feel that he deserved it.

I came home two weeks later to finish recuperating. But, interestingly, my parents always insisted that I return to that same HMO doctor. I'm sure they felt this particular physician would be especially careful not to miss another obvious diagnosis like a ruptured appendix. But after a week in ICU, I had never wanted to see the man again. How could they think of taking me back to him?

A few years later, though, I learned that drugs I only knew by street names – "reds" or "black beauties" – were actually prescription medicines. If I could figure out what they were, I could get them from this doctor who knew he had dodged a losing lawsuit in his lack of treatment for my appendicitis. He was therefore especially compliant with any request I had.

# 3
# SUICIDE PLANS

Home was unbearable by the time I was 14. I knew I had no power in my own life. Trying to work on anything with my parents was out of the question. My mother had started to drink even more and my father had taken a new tack with the fighting and bitterness at home. He started telling me, "You're the center of this, you know. You're the center of the problems in our family."

I did not realize then that this was a common way dysfunctional families behave. The child who is more functional than the parents is given all the responsibilities and blame for everything. It was a hard role to be cast into, but there was one big blessing. Being 14 and overweight, I was falling out of my father's sick attraction range. This protected me from his sexual obsessions, but not from his overall cruelty. I stood up to him from time to time and took the lashings – physical or verbal – with an ill-begotten stoicism.

Wendy would try to tell me, "No, when they spank you, you need to cry out – really loud, louder than you think you should – that makes them stop sooner." She tried to teach me the "Br'er Rabbit" tricks – "Oh, don't make me go to my room and read a book (something I LOVED to do)," etc. She seemed to pull them off with aplomb.

It was good that Wendy had that ability, and of course I still worked my hardest to protect her. For instance, if chores were given, I took the outdoor ones. I knew that's where my father would be. I'd be mowing, or trimming trees or fixing the fence and it took nothing at all to set my father off. Something would go awry – he was hit in the shin by a plank we were carrying or a branch from the tree hit his eye – and the bellowing would begin. Wolf eyes appeared and suddenly I was the center of the problem.

When bickering started at the dinner table – my mother wasn't fast enough to refill his coffee cup or she undercooked the roast – it was my fault for not helping her more. If she drank her booze, it was my fault for worrying her with some misbehavior.

At about that age, I had also started to realize that I did not have the same feelings my friends did about boys. Most of the time, I was completely baffled by my friends' new behavior. Why did they act differently when a boy walked up? Why were they trying to get attention from them?

Being a bit of a loner, I started my search in the public library. I had to sneak into the part where grade school kids were not allowed, and through a long search I finally found a book that described my feelings and gave advice about it. Back then they thought homosexuality was a disorder. If you felt you had this syndrome, you should talk to "your minister or school nurse."
Now that was puzzling. What on earth did those two have in common? I still remember the school nurse; a white-haired lady with ringlets pinned to her head with dozens of white bobby pins. I went once to try to talk to her about my new and confusing feelings. I never said why I was there, and after lots of stuttering, I asked for an aspirin and left. It was probably for the best given the times and my situation.

I think the hardest thing for me to endure with my father was when he pulled off cruelty to my mother with people watching him. For instance, we'd had a huge battle one morning over my mother not refilling his coffee cup soon enough. He'd shoved her into the service table, raging that she did nothing right. That same night, as she served company, my father had his jolly goodness act going. He was gregarious and entertaining to the guests. The very moment one of them finished their coffee he jumped to his feet to refill the cup. My mother tried to beat him to the coffee pot, but with her bruised ribs and back she couldn't move quickly. My father, knowing her intentions, would say "Oh no, Winna. You have a seat, *dear*. Let ME get that coffee cup refilled for our friends." So everyone left saying, "Wow, that Ed. What a great guy, isn't he?"

I knew differently, but I felt silenced by the continual blame I was given when anything went wrong during that first year of high school. It was almost a refrain that ended any conversation with me, "And you know, you are the center of the problems in this family."

Toward the end of my freshman year, I got to school early one morning, stolen cigarettes in my purse, and went to the girls' room to wait for the cool girls I wanted to be accepted by. They were the ones who rebelled against authority figures and boldly denied having cigarettes while the smoke was still strong on their breath.

Dale, a friend I related to because she had been adopted and abused, stuck her head in and said hello, but I barely acknowledged her. I was waiting for The Group. Finally, the gang rounded the corner of the room. The girls at the back of the pack shouted, "Is anybody in there?" The two girls in front looked right at me and shouted back, "Nope, no one's here. Let's go somewhere else," and they left. I actually knew that they had not even meant to be unkind. It was simply true in their eyes. I was no one to them.

I was not really one of the gang at all and I felt like a "no one" inside my own mind, too. There was a new counselor on campus that held some weekly group meetings. You had to be interviewed to get into the group. We never knew if you had to be bad enough or good enough or just be the best storyteller to get in, but the real status of the counselor's group was that he let us out of a class and allowed smoking during group. Getting in was a highly coveted position. I had managed to get into the counseling group, but it was sort of a personal dare. I wanted to say I got to smoke on campus, but I did not like the counselor. I'll call him Dr. Bennett. He seemed very full of himself. I almost want to say he was "preachy" but that's not quite right. He just sort of summed you up, told you "the truth" about yourself and sat back like he'd won a game. He was not really the approachable type.

In the middle of all this, my father got a big acknowledgment. He was given an award by Los Angeles County for his wonderful work in the probation department, as I recall. It was covered in local newspapers and people would talk to me about it. "Wow, you must be so proud of your father," "Hey I read about your Dad – guess he's a real hero."

My mother, in spite of her drinking, remained a well-thought-of teacher and well-loved choir director at church. My kid sister had tons of friends – and tried her best to share them with me since I had very few. Loneliness can amplify pain.

All these things confirmed in my 14-year-old mind that I must really be the center of the problem in my family. I began to plan a way to end my life. At first, I wanted it to look like an accident. I didn't have a driver's license, so that ruled out running into a light pole. I tried loosely tying my sneakers together and running down the stairs, hoping they'd be just tight enough to trip me and just loose enough not to be obvious when I was found. I fell several times, but could not imagine this working well. I tried riding my bike in traffic, but when a woman slammed on her brakes to miss me, I saw the look of panic in her face and realized I could not do this to someone else. I should be the only one hurt. I knew that some people did drugs, but I had no idea where to find the illegal ones at the time.

I still have several scars from small attempts at cutting myself with a razor blade, something I had done to externalize my pain for years. This was long before they labeled people who did that as "cutters." I could never get very deep with it and I was afraid I'd be found and saved before I died. Killing oneself is not easy.

Then I remembered my father's gun. Wendy and I had long known the hiding place which was in a back corner of his top closet shelf in a shoe box. I had also found the bullets, which he kept separately in a sock drawer. That gave me a quick and presumably painless means, but how could I do it and be sure (in my own mind anyway) to only be hurting myself? Shooting myself at school was out of the question. What if I hit someone else? I couldn't do it at home because I would never take the chance that my sister or my mother would find me.

The golf course across the street from the school was a possibility, but the caretaker of the grounds there was a nice little old man and

I didn't want to give him a heart attack if he found my body. Then the golf course hired a sort of a crass, smart aleck young man on Mondays and Tuesdays. I couldn't imagine he would give a hoot about finding a body on his watch, and the noise of a gun would make it pretty certain that he would be the first one to get there.

So, the how and where were taken care of. Now came the 'when.' I wanted to be sure that everyone's last memory of me was a happy one. I had a speech contest coming up the following weekend. It was near the campus where a favorite camp counselor lived in the dorms. I always had crushes on the young women who were my summer camp counselors and would carry their pictures all year long. I figured in the next two weeks, I could sort of see or speak to everyone important to me and have lovely conversations for them to remember.

I could see my camp counselor once more, call my half-brother to say how much I loved him and be sure to be extra nice to Wendy. I carefully wrote out little notes to everyone I could think of, saying something kind and assuring them that my actions were not their fault – it was just that I was the center of the problems in my family.

What followed were the calmest, happiest days of my adolescence. I felt completely at peace knowing I had the solution to the problem. I was ardently aware of being nice and kind to everyone. I had made a decision and it felt right. I got my father's gun down and figured out how to load it, and then carefully put everything back. I tucked all the notes in my purse where I was sure they would be found immediately after I shot myself. It seemed everything was in place. The following Monday would be the day.

Just after the little notes were written, Dale was in the girls' room with me at school and borrowed my lipstick. I left for the next class and in the middle of the class was summoned to my favorite teacher's office. I tended to develop crushes on teachers, too, so being called to Mrs. Page's office was kind of cool.

I was still in my bubble of feeling that all I had to do was get through the next few days and then all of my problems…including me… would be gone. I had no foreboding heading for her office. I opened the door and was all the way inside before I saw that it was Dr. Bennett waiting for me in my teacher's office. My teacher moved between me and the door and I could feel my world collapsing. Dr. Bennett very calmly said, "So, I understand you plan to kill yourself next Monday."

I can't begin to describe the feelings that went through me. For the next hour I felt like I was drowning in the rapids and grasping for one branch after another that kept breaking off in my hands. Dr. Bennett was so arrogant and proud of how cool he was that I couldn't imagine he had answers for me, but my teacher was there too, so I had the fleeting thought that maybe this would all mean I could get help; that someone could fix me or put our family together in a way that allowed us all to survive, so I sat down. While my head was racing to figure out what he knew and how much he knew, he just stared at me. I'm sure he was thinking that I was being a sullen, silent teenager, but I simply had no idea what to say. Part of me wished hard that I had the moxie to say, "Yep, I am, so I guess you can count me out for group next week. Bye!"

But instead, for one moment I let my guard down and tried to think of how to ask for help. I felt certain his next question would be about why I planned it or what was wrong or could he help. Instead he asked, "Who is going to be the most injured by your suicide?"

I had to think about that. *My kid sister? My half- brother?* Certainly not my father who would no doubt be relieved, I thought. Finally, I said, "I guess my Mom would be."

"Well, now that we know that you're doing this to hurt your mother, let's talk about other people in your family." I saw my hands grow white, my feet got cold, and finally so numb that I knew I couldn't run.

He continued, "I understand your Dad is a pretty great guy. He's even won awards for helping young people. Surely you could talk with him if you were that upset. Tell me some of the

33

good things about your father." I was flummoxed. I had certainly never felt the intent to hurt my mother and the thought that he would no doubt pass that "information" on horrified me. But all that he had to say about my father was like being in the middle of some bad horror movie where everyone in the whole movie turns out to be the monster and no matter where you turn, there he is, the same monster in another form.

I began to insanely babble, "Oh yeah, my Dad, he's great. Did you see all that about him in the newspaper? Oh sure, I could talk to him about anything. He's won so many awards and he loves to do things with me – takes me camping and fishing."

Suddenly a light bulb in my benumbed brain finally flickered on "Oh, You're probably just talking about those silly notes in my purse that Dale must have found. That was kind of a mean trick to let my friend think they were real. They were just some things a bunch of us wrote at a slumber party about what our last words would be and what we'd want people to know if anything ever happened to us. I definitely should have told Dale it was a joke. Gosh, I'm sorry, about that."

My teacher looked relieved, but Dr. Bennett clearly was not buying the "it was a joke" part. He plowed on through a few more coolly phrased questions and just about the time I thought for sure I had him convinced he said, "Well, I've written a note home to your parents. It explains what's been going on and what the school will do about it."

When I looked blank, he picked up a paper and read, "Dear Mr. and Mrs. Carter, this is to inform you that your daughter, Marsha, plans to kill herself on Monday May 22. Please understand she will not be allowed to attend school that day and will need a psychologist's or psychiatrist's release to return. Sincerely, Dr. Bennett, School Psychologist."

My utter horror at the wording of the letter was only mitigated by my wild hope that this meant he had not mailed it yet and I could somehow offer to take it home myself. He saw through that in an instant and said, "This is a copy. The original has been sent."

I looked at my teacher still leaning on the door. "Am I allowed to leave now?" To me her face looked compassionate and as though she was just about to say something else to me. Then she gave a questioning glance to Dr. Bennett who nodded, and she moved away from the door.

I left immediately. The most instantly crushing thing was that all my wonderful feelings of certitude and benevolence had vanished. Part of it was Dr. Bennett's utter disconnectedness. He wrote about me with all the concern of an overdue library book notice. He seemed far more cunning than caring – I couldn't imagine treating people the way he was treating my parents.

But it also shed light on my own actions. Just like someone having an illicit affair with a coworker might feel it was exciting, invigorating and beautifully sensual until they are discovered. Then once it is revealed, it simply seems tawdry and self-destructive and it means the loss of family, job and respect. I stepped far enough outside of my teenage skin for just a moment to realize the pain that I would cause.

Then I leapt back into simply trying to minimize the damage and stay out of trouble. The first and most immediate problem was the letter, of course. I didn't dare miss school on Thursday – the day I expected it to arrive. Fortunately, my sister did not attend this school. I was in 9th grade but she was in 6th. Dr. Bennett had not mentioned her in the session, so I had some hope that no one would think of whether she missed school on Thursday. I told Wendy that it was a note that was going to get me in trouble and she just had to stay home and retrieve it for me. Ever the loving and acquiescent kid sister, she did.

The next problem was convincing Dale that it was all a joke. I have to say that as much as I blathered on with one excuse after another, she never bought a word of it. I think we both lived in our own solitary worlds of pain. She was just more sensitive than I was, and stronger. At least, she tried to reach out.

When the weekend came without incident I thought I'd escaped the wrath of my father and pain of my mother. Just as I was supposed to leave for the speech contest, my father called me into the living room. I'm not really sure who called him to be certain that they had received "the letter," nor do I remember if they ever read the awful thing. My father's chief concerns seemed to be that I'd inconvenienced so many people with my attention-getting and that now he and my mother would have to take me to a therapist before I could return to school. Then he allowed me to go to the speech contest over the weekend. Again I was floored. I thought at least my mother would insist I stay home and get help.

I tried several times to get the feeling again – that "everything will be over soon" placid air that I'd lost. I also stood alone in my father's bedroom with the loaded gun pointed at my head, hoping that even if I couldn't pull the trigger; my finger might twitch and make the choice for me.

Instead I trudged to the two-day speech contest. I did get to see my camp counselor, but here she was in a very different light. Rather than being up in the mountains in a cabin caring for a bunch of girls, she was a college student whose weekend I was interrupting. I left as quickly as I could and prepared for Monday and the visit with the psychiatrist my parents had hired.

We pulled up to his office and all went in at first. Once more I had the insanity of hoping for help. Just before the doctor opened the door my father said, "He is very well thought of in the area. He works with me." Again I felt that "the monsters are everywhere" nightmare. The doctor suggested that he speak with me for as long as we needed to, then he'd call my parents back in. Knowing that he worked with my award-winning father, I put on the fairytales again. It had been a joke. It was stuff from a slumber party. It was all just a big misunderstanding. He asked me if I had been serious, how I would imagine that I would kill myself.

I said with a gun. He asked if my father had a gun (I guess in those days one did not think about whether one's mother had a gun). I said he did. He asked if I knew where it was. I hedged. "It's probably in his room somewhere." As he honed in on the questions, I denied ever seeing it and certainly wouldn't know how to shoot it.

Finally, I said, "Well maybe I was a little down but I'm all better now. You know, I'm like one of those tough little Super Balls (a novelty in that era) – I just bounce higher every time." He was quiet for a moment, and then said, "Did you know that if you bounce a super ball hard enough, it explodes?"

I walked out to the car. I sat there, waiting for my parents to emerge. They were in there far longer than I thought it would take to get a synopsis of all that I had said. Some distant part of my heart still fluttered with the last breath of a hope that something would change, that we would get help – before my mother drank herself to death or my father killed her, before I left my sister at his mercy by abandoning her with my suicide, before every adult turned into the monster.

My parents returned to the car smiling and I heard the doctor call out, "OK, I'll see you." I thought perhaps we were returning before I realized he just meant he'd see my Dad at the office.
My father turned to me and said (whether it was true or not, I'll never know), "Well, we had a great talk, dear. We talked over a great many things…and he says you are the center of the problems in this family."

The last flutter of hope gasped and died; I bought my first drugs the next day.

# 4

# DRUGS

L ife on drugs seemed much easier at first. I finally really did have a group to hang out with. I was thrilled (if you can even imagine saying these words with a straight face) to be a doper. The sayings of the day, "Don't trust anyone over 30" made perfect sense to me, as did "Turn on, tune in and drop out."

I think I already weighed close to 200 pounds in my early high school years, so clearly I needed to lose weight and dextroamphetamine was a perfectly legal diet pill, known as 'black beauties' on the street. The doctor prescribed them for me each time I asked and I loved the rush from the speed. It pulled me out of my doldrums and depression and made me exciting and outgoing and happy. Of course, they are terribly addictive, but I didn't really care. I would have used anything to feel better.

For the next two years I tried to style myself as a hippie. It seemed bold and daring and very cool. It helped that a lot of kids called me "Mama Cass" because I was heavy and I sang. Although I was sort of mortified the first time I heard it, I realized it was actually meant to be a compliment. I was not allowed to listen to the Mamas and the Papas at home. My parents forbade listening to "rock and roll" because *that* was immoral.

They tried buying me LP's (old fashioned black vinyl discs played at 33 1/3 revolutions a minute) of what they considered appropriate music. I could not bear to listen to most of what they brought home - the sappy, clean-cut young people singing meaningless lyrics, but I secretly sort of liked Mitch Miller and the Gang when they sang folk songs from long ago. Fortunately for me, Peter, Paul and Mary also called themselves folk singers and had one of the same songs on their LP that Mitch Miller did, so they slid by my parent's restrictions, along with Simon and Garfunkel.

The dean of girls called me in when my grades dropped. I could see her trying to get through to me, but I really didn't care. She closed the door to her office and in a lowered voice said, "Did they talk to you about your IQ tests in junior high?" I shook my head. I barely remembered taking the tests in the 8th grade. "I know I'm not supposed to tell you this, but you have the highest IQ in the school, Marsha. You have so much potential."

I laughed. "You bet. I am just full of potential. I'd be so pretty if only I wasn't fat and I'd be so smart if only I applied myself. I have news for you, potential is nothing. When I die, my potential is going straight to hell with me."

I took my journal to the football field, smoked a joint and wrote a gloomy poem about potential. The only thing that cheered me was that I spent as much time as I could with my half-brother that summer when I was turning 15. I knew he was a "real hippie" and that he'd gotten into trouble dropping acid with the infamous Harvard psychologist Timothy Leary when he was in New York, so I thought he was just the coolest person I knew.

Charles turned out to be a very noble drug abuser; he would not supply me with any drugs, but he would take them with me if I brought them. An interesting boundary, I thought. I had no desire for alcohol because of my parents' drinking, but I did come to realize that Charles drank and that made me sad. We figured out how to hide drugs in my purse in places where my parents never searched. If you've never looked inside your daughter's tampon holder, take my word for it – no one looks in there.

I always admired Charles. He was my hero in so many ways. He was brilliant, having received multiple scholarships to pay his way through college, graduate school and earn a doctorate in physics from the Rockefeller Institute. He loved my mother, stood up to our father with complete and confident self-assurance. To top it off, he adored me.

One time when we were playing the game, 'Truth or Dare,' and he asked me, "Honestly, when you're all alone in the bathroom looking in the mirror, don't you really know that you are pretty?" I was stunned and chose the "Dare," but the wonder has never left me. My big brother thought I was pretty!

There was also a lot of whispering done in our house about Charles. I knew, of course, that he took drugs. I assumed that most of the clandestine meetings about him had to do with that. It was not until much later, when another family member had asked me, "You know about Charles, right?" I had nodded affirmatively – not because I was sure that I knew anything, but because I wanted them to continue. They went on about the man he was living with and how sad it was to "think he was homosexual."

I was shocked, but I didn't really think of him as "being like me" in any way. I was sure that I would grow out of my attraction to other girls (the book had said so). People also talked about the "reasons" someone like Charles was gay - for instance, because his parents were divorced when he was in puberty. I'm not sure how much my parents knew about Charles' sexuality, but they were very familiar with his drug use. As I recall, they ended up paying the bills for some damages he did at Rockefeller while he was there. But in spite of their best attempts to keep most of our get-togethers tightly supervised, Charles and I usually managed to run off for a walk in the park or even the occasional camping excursion. It was the best part of any trip.

Charles was always looking out for Wendy and me. One day, in the spring of 1969 when I was sixteen, he got us a singing job. It was a real gig. To be sure my 13-year-old sister and I had been singing all of our lives. We sang together playing in the backyard; we were hauled out to perform for every visiting friend or relative. We had even made spending money together as wandering minstrels in a local restaurant. But this was different.

My groovy older brother had gotten us a gig at a coffeehouse at a local college. Growing up in Claremont, California, colleges were common. There were seven in town. Charles had graduated from Pomona College a few years earlier and still had friends and connections there. He was in the audience to hear us. So, disconcertingly, was my mother. She later commented that she didn't know girls smoked pipes. She had no clue what people were smoking in those pipes.

Wendy and I had practiced every Peter, Paul & Mary and Simon & Garfunkel song we knew on guitar. We watched the group ahead of us and saw that, although a very few people still snapped their fingers fifties-style, most applauded – a signal, I suppose, that the beatniks had given way to hippies. Then it was our turn ... and I froze.

*Flashback: Remembering Summer Camp*
*This freezing and nerves had been solidified at summer camp. My best friend Audrey and I went every year. This past year had been exceptionally intense. While in previous years our parents may have been able to afford one or two weeks for us, this year Audrey and I found that if we volunteered to work with younger campers we could go several weeks for free. This meant hours together talking long into the night.*

*I was amazed that Audrey liked me, especially that she considered me her best friend. Everyone liked Audrey. She was tall, thin and had long, curly red hair. She could wear a miniskirt and look fantastic. And, of course, all of her miniskirts seemed to be handmade from hand woven fabric. Her long freckled legs folded every which way, but always seemed to look comfortable. She was able to engage in conversation with anyone – especially the boys.*

*I tagged along. I learned to disappear when her demeanor with a boy became different, and reappear when she was ready to spend time with me again. This never bothered me; it was just part of the rhythm of our relationship. Whenever Audrey was off with a boy, I played my guitar.*

*But this past summer, Audrey had appeared pale and wan, thinner* than ever and more raggedly dressed. People openly commented on her appearance, asked about her, and spoke to her, but I was her sole confidante. I knew what had really happened. Her mother had left her father when she discovered that he was molesting Audrey. Then when she found that Audrey was pregnant by an older boyfriend, she had taken Audrey to Mexico for an abortion.

I won't go into the horrific details, but it was the most traumatizing experience of her life and Audrey had shared it with me. She had almost died from infection and blood loss. We talked, cried, and wrote in our journals. We wrote poems and sang songs. But Audrey had told no one else.

My big plans for camp that year had been to learn a new song on the guitar. I wanted to sing at the talent show and be good at something. Every year the camp counselors attempted to let each of us know how special we were. One of the ways they did that was to divide us into groups and give us a list of attributes. Then each group competed. Who had the longest eyelashes? Had the biggest eyes? Who could sing the highest note? Who has the darkest skin or the lightest? The idea was for each camper to find an area at which they excelled or in which they were unique.

I had never found one.

Some people thought singing the highest note might be my forte, but what that actually involved was squealing. Since no one could distinguish between squealing and singing, the highest squealer was the one who inevitably won that round.

So this year I had practiced for hours. My fingertips were raw from playing the guitar chords over and over again. I think it was The Times They Are a Changin' by Bob Dylan. At any rate, the long awaited night of the talent show had arrived. I was the last act. I couldn't believe it; I was going to be best at something.

I managed to get through the song with no mistakes. I even had a partial standing ovation. But then the camp counselor announced *that he had one more participant he wanted to include. Audrey stood on stage. In a halting voice she shared the very short version of what had happened to her. Then she began to sing. No music. No accompaniment and to be honest, very few notes.*

*Audrey sang out in a loud trembling voice, To Dream the Impossible Dream. She changed keys a dozen times. She missed words or made up her own. But the other campers were on their feet, cheering her on and on, running to her on the stage to hug her toward the end. This was the 60s and it was the decade of sensitivity sessions and making it real. It was all about baring your heart. People were more impressed because she couldn't sing, but she did it anyway.*

*I loved Audrey, I still do. The response she received was surely therapeutic for her. But I still hurt inside. I left there with the feeling that I would never be best at anything.*

*** 

So here I was now at the coffee house with my kid sister, and I choked. I could not open my mouth to sing. I could feel my throat closing. Quickly glancing at our song list, I chose a song that required my sister to start. I pointed to it and started the chords for that song. Ever the compliant kid sister, Wendy's sweet voice rang out and I managed to chime in with harmony by the chorus. My brother, Charles, sent loud "bravos" from the crowd. Others clapped – or snapped – and we finished our set.

After the show, Charles stayed to talk to us. With my mother present, he invited us to "something exciting going on down at the beach." My face fell. I knew the answer would be no. There was no way my mother was going to let me go to a party an hour away "at the beach" with my sometimes troublesome big brother. To my amazement my mother said yes and arrangements were made for Charles to pick us up the next Monday night.

Wendy and I were long accustomed to being asked to sing almost everywhere we went, so we brought along a guitar. We were picturing bonfires and partiers on the beach, but Charles took us to an upstairs room in a restaurant near Huntington Beach.

It was full of hippies, my half-sister Kay was there, and everyone seemed very religious. Wendy and I changed gears. It seemed we were going to have to perform something from church rather than a folksong. We huddled quickly. What hymns did we know on the guitar? Did we know any songs that were religious? Wait! I knew a Rod McKuen song that mentioned Jesus in the second verse. Running quickly over the chords we sat down with the group. As they assembled we heard young people talking about Jesus as though He were still alive. They chit-chatted amiably, as if He was one of the group, "Jesus told me to go to her house," Or "Jesus let me know I had to pray about that and I let go of it." along with "Jesus gave me the sign I was looking for."

I wondered briefly if they had a youth pastor named Jesús - like a Latino name. But it was pretty clear they were talking about "the" Jesus. The one whom I clearly remembered died about 2000 years ago. I felt as though I had walked into a science-fiction movie. Surely these normal, seemingly intelligent people did not believe He was still alive. My brother! My big brother! Could he believe that a Jesus who lived 2,000 years ago was still alive? It reminded me of a science fiction story I'd read about Lazarus, the guy Jesus raised from the dead, still being alive.

As the meeting drew together and introductions were made, Charles introduced Wendy and me. He shared that we were singers and we pulled out the guitar. We stumbled our way through the classic hymn, "How Great Thou Art." Then we begin to sing "Suzanne" by the great songwriter, Leonard Cohen. Perhaps you remember that haunting and poetic lyric:

"Suzanne takes you down to a place by the river, you can hear the boats go by; you can spend the night forever…"

Well, the second verse had something about Jesus in it. We thought that should be sufficient. Apparently it was not. A young hippie with shoulder-length hair named Lonnie Frisbee stood up. "Jesus was not a sailor and He did not say the sea would free you. He said He would set you free," Lonnie stated boldly.

'Whatever!' I thought. I was mildly annoyed that he did not approve of the song. I had no way of knowing he would be THE main preacher among what was about to explode across the nation as "The Jesus Movement" (Jesus freaks).

The evening continued and included a video where Pat Boone was trying to speak to college students about God. Mr. Boone attempted to use vernacular, telling the students earnestly that Jesus was groovy; that they would dig his far out teachings and He would heal them from drug addiction.

Clearly Pat Boone did not know that we - the hip generation- did not take drugs to get high. In the '60's we took drugs to expand our minds. Between segments of Mr. Boone's discussions of religion, girls in white boots appeared on the video singing, "who's tripping down the streets of the city...." It seemed to me that Jesus was not interesting enough to keep us watching the video without dancing go-go girls.

I thought very little about the evening except that I was disappointed with my brother for sneaking me out to church. I had been ready for a party. Some people tried to talk to us afterward, but we were embarrassed that our song had been deemed inappropriate. We shook our heads on the way home – what nutcases!

After all, we went to church too, you know. We heard all about the cross where Jesus DIED. Of course we remembered all the stuff about how He went to heaven afterward or whatever, but nothing about Him being here now. That was no more real than the Easter bunny or the Tooth Fairy.

I remembered someone saying "Jesus died for your sins," and I found that odd, too. What a thing to say! "I love my kids so much I would die for them and..." what? Jesus loved my sins so much

He would die for them? What kind of sense did that make? Plus, seriously, who wanted to be like those dancing girls? I honestly hadn't known Pat Boone was still living (although in future years he became a sweet friend and he is alive at the writing of this book in his 80's).

My week went on and I often thought about my disappointment with the event at the beach. What had my brother thought I'd get out of that? Was he worried about the dope I smoked occasionally? I did some pot, fiddled around very little with hallucinogens, and took speed whenever I could find it to try to deal with my weight and depression.

I also had the perfect boyfriend. Pat lived about 2 ½ hours away where we visited my Aunt Polly twice a year. I could show his picture to everyone and share his occasional letters to prove I had a boyfriend – he even showed up once at a school dance – but mostly it meant I never had to deal with the boys at home or dating anyone else. After all, I had a boyfriend. Case closed.

My boyfriend and I did drugs every time we were together, and each visit grew predictably more progressive. We started out smoking pot. The next visit no one had that, so we bought hashish. The next time we got pills ("black beauties" and "rainbows" as I recall) and so on. My brother Charles had done a lot more than that. He even drank alcohol. Yet, he was worried about me and he was about to bring me to a place where my life would change forever.

# 5
# JESUS AT THE BEACH & CALVARY CHAPEL

I was lying in bed the week after Charles took us to the "something exciting going on down at the beach" event. The nightly rumbles between my parents had begun. My father was in my mother's bedroom going through drawers, trying to find where she hid alcohol or pills. My mother somehow drew him out of her room, then ran in and locked the door behind her. The banging and shouting and raging set in. I pulled the covers over my head.

Here I was 16 years old and I still prayed what I had for years; that I would suffocate in the night... and never wake up here again. Somewhere in the back of my mind a thought flickered. *What a trip it would be to feel like those people at the beach. To believe Jesus would really talk to me? To think that Jesus cared whose house I went to. Weirdos.*

The thought impelled me through the week. I was taking speed every morning, which made me friendlier at school, but not more popular. I was dumpy, and stoned most of the time, or smoking in the girls' room.

My sweet boyfriend, Pat, had taken the train up to see me. When he disembarked in 90-degree weather wearing a shirt with long sleeves, I knew instantly that he had graduated to IV drugs. He was hiding the track marks on his arms, and I would not follow him there.

Most of high school had been fairly miserable for me. I had tried every trick I knew to try to be accepted and popular. I had parties where literally no one came. I tried Girl Scouts mistakenly thinking that it would be fun to do outdoor excursions like Boy Scouts. I loved camping and fishing, building fires and archery. Girl Scouts turned out, in the case of our town anyway, to be various ways of setting the table, doing craft projects and styling clothing outfits which was the worst of all. Oh misery. This, of course, involved taking one's measurements. It was so not happening. I probably hovered between 200 and 250 pounds for most of high school. I was quite self-conscious enough without anyone taking my measurements.

I wasn't quite book-smart enough to fit in with the straight-A kids. I certainly wasn't athletic enough to befriend the jocks and, although I could sing, I knew nothing really about music so I couldn't hang with the band geeks. As I said, I thought that if I could abscond with a couple of cigarettes out of my dad's pack every day, the girls who smoked in the bathroom would hang out with me.

Not only was I overweight, but even my feet were bigger than anyone else's in my class. I finally found a fairly authentic pair of moccasins that fit. They were white soft leather with a fringe. No real soles, no decorations, just leather that wrapped my feet. Some of the bathroom gang thought they were cool, so I loved them – wore 'em all the time. Then came one of the very few rainy days in Southern California. It was to bring the kind of embarrassment that still makes my face burn many years later.

We had a food court at my school. There were perhaps 8 or 10 machines that stocked food for our lunches. A couple of the machines dispensed hot food, others salty snacks and others sweet stuff. One had juice and a couple had sodas. As you can imagine, my choices were less than healthy. Generally, I got a hot pastrami sandwich, Fritos and a soda ... then tried to sit somewhere unobtrusive in the lunch area to eat.

On this particular day, the rain started while I was in the food court area. I got my food and started to run quickly through the rain to a covered area with tables. The moccasins became an instant liability because they were just soft leather skidding on water. I slipped helplessly to my bum on the rain-drenched cement. It smarted. I tried to stand while a couple of people laughed, but my feet could not find traction. I just kept slipping and sliding. I was first on my knees, then on my behind, and finally on my back. The longer I tried to get up, the more people gathered to laugh. By this point I had completely dropped my food, focusing only on getting to my feet and out of there. Students started pointing out my food and making comments about whether I should be eating those things. I slipped once more.

Ultimately, I had to sit in the rain, unlace and take off my moccasins to be able to stand up and walk out of vision-range of the hysterical crowd. I was crushed that not one person had helped me. And I was mortified. I never wore the evil moccasins again. After that, I went early to buy my food and took it into a bathroom stall to eat or under the bleachers on the football field. That way, no one could see that I ate alone and no one could see or comment on what I ate.

I could sing however, so the nicer kids focused on that. The other place I had excelled was at speech contests, and that was generally when they had a category called "Oratorical Interpretation". This was a fancy way of saying "quoting poetry," which I loved. The only people to hang out with during speech contests, however, were the debate team brainiacs. Although none of us would have said it at the time, they were actually my best friends.

I remember I asked one of them, Alisa, if she had ever heard of anyone who thought Jesus was still alive. She looked at me like I had two heads, and walked off. In hindsight, given that Alisa is Jewish, maybe she wasn't the best person to ask, but she was smart and I thought she'd know. (She's still one of the few friends I have who can stump me at online word games.)

One of the great things about being 16 was being able to drive, or at least having a license. I'd been driving since I was a little kid in a pickup truck in the lemon groves, slogging one mile-per-hour down each row as my father threw fertilizer bags off the back of the truck bed to the itinerant workers. But at 16, when that next Monday night came, I hopped in my car alone and headed for the beach for another evening church gathering.

I stopped at my brother's house first to let him know I was coming. He told me they were meeting at a new building that was going to be called Calvary Chapel. Of course, their new building had not yet been built. So we were actually meeting on the concrete slab that had been poured for the building.

It was perfect for meeting outside in California in early June. As kids began to gather I brought the ashtray from my car onto the concrete slab, noticing they didn't have one. As wildly inappropriate as that may have seemed to any regular churchgoing people, no one seemed offended. Someone quietly thanked me, but pointed out that this was going to be a "sanctuary", a "safe place," so no one would be smoking in this area. They were casual and sweet, and I was glad for the tip. I tucked the ashtray into my purse.

This week there were no special presentations like there had been the week before when my brother brought me. There was no one to put on a show and no movies to watch. People just talked about what God had done in their lives that week. They talked about successes and failures and seemed certain that Jesus had helped them over rough spots or encouraged them when they needed it.

The pastor, Chuck Smith, gave a Bible study. He talked about Jesus standing at the door of one's heart and knocking. He called Jesus a "gentleman, who would not come in without being invited." The idea of someone with boundaries sounded good to me. He also said that Jesus had been through everything that we go through, so He understood us. I really listened when he said that He would never leave us or forsake us.

Even as I write these things, I understand how hackneyed they can sound to some people who have heard them repeated into meaninglessness all of their lives. But what I'd heard about Jesus before was that He was this really nice guy, who lived a long time ago. He told us to "do unto others as we would have others do unto us," had long hair and wore sandals. He would have fit the 1960's well. I knew He tragically died young and went up into heaven. Anything else I'd heard about Him I had filed away with other made-up stories.

I was unnerved at the end of the service when they all gathered in a circle to pray. First of all, they didn't pray in the terminology and style I was accustomed to: "Oh great and mighty God, we beseech Thee that Thou wouldst be in our midst." God had always seemed so far away and uninvolved to me.

Instead they actually seemed to be chatting with God – and it was not just the pastor or Lonnie Frisbee, the youth leader that talked that way. (It seems kind of funny because Lonnie would NEVER have called himself the "youth pastor" but that was my terminology at the time.) Everybody prayed as they went around the circle and talked just like they would have talked to any friend. When they got to me I just blurted out, "Oh God, please accept me into Thy fold!" My face flushed with embarrassment.

There was no big reaction from anyone. Others just finished praying and we walked outside. I remember looking up in the sky to see a falling star and starting to "make a wish" on it, when I thought, *"Maybe I should just pray about it instead."* Whoa. *Where did that thought come from?* I always wished on falling stars. A woman named Lorna asked if some of us would like to come over after church. I was already going to be late and in trouble when I got home, so I thought – *in for a penny, in for a pound,* and headed over to her place.

At Lorna and Bill's house someone finally asked me what I had meant by my prayer. Had I decided I wanted to know Jesus? I started to cry and I remember saying, "I'm just so full of foolish pride." Even in my own 16-year-old ears at the time, that sounded so ... old. But I knew there was no way in the world I was just going to go home and suddenly "be good" and be a Christian. Lorna said, "That's not how it works at all. If you were already everything you wanted to be and everything you needed to be, you wouldn't need Jesus anyway."

Other people, including my half-sister, Kay, who had been milling around, stopped to tune in. Someone offered to lead me in "the sinner's prayer," but I was already on my knees and praying.

For those who are keeping track, I did, specifically, ask Jesus to forgive my sins – the ones I knew about and the ones I didn't. I asked Him to come into my heart, to show me that He was real. I gave my life to Him.

I also asked for the power of the Holy Spirit to be able live as a Christian, since I couldn't even begin to picture what that would look like on me. I said as much and Lorna told me it was the Holy Spirit who gave us the power to live, learning to follow Christ. To my great good fortune, no one made any doctrinal statements about what I did or didn't have to do. They just told me that Jesus said even we know how to give good gifts to our children, so how much more would a loving God give the Holy Spirit to whomever asked … and I asked.

The first thing that happened was that I suddenly felt that all the arms that were around me just then were somehow Jesus' arms. I'd seen pictures of Jesus with little kids in His lap and I felt like I was one of them. It seemed so solid and real that years later when a friend made me a small sculpture of the scene I told her, "I was on His other knee."

Most of all, it seemed to me that Jesus was big enough to contain all of us; to contain me and my world. Then I saw a huge crashing river. Let me say here that I understand how bizarre this all sounds to some people. I also understand where some writers in the Bible say, "Whether I was really there or it was a vision, I don't know." 2 Corinthians 12:3 KJV

It seemed real to me and I could feel the spray of the water. I remember realizing that with this much water none of us should have to be thirsty. I was thinking of inner thirst and I related that to nighttime at my house. That habit of hiding under the covers, hoping to suffocate in the night and not have to "wake up here" again had started very young. This was the thirst in my life – the endless tears, fears and failures of those nights. Jesus looked down at me and said, "I was there every night. I felt every tear. That's why I died."

I want to be clear that I'm not trying to write new doctrine here. In the Old Testament, there are   many descriptive names for the one God. They were words added to God's name to talk about how God meets our needs. One was Jehovah-Jireh, meaning "God, the provider" or "God who has become all that I need." I believe that's what Jesus was doing in that moment – meeting me at my need. I can tell you that it literally rewrote my entire life.

My mind flew back to a thousand moments when someone, some thought, some action, some feeling had saved me or taken me from a dangerous or painful situation, and I thought, "That was YOU." Nothing from that moment when I was 16 years old was ever the same again. It changed my perspective of everything that had happened in my life even before that day to realize that Jesus hadn't waited for me to get it right, or believe the right doctrines, or understand the right theology. Jesus had been there all along. It also created a deep faith for me. I knew from that moment on that there was a part of me that was permanently safe.

I've often wished since then that I could share that gift or impart it to someone else. Certainly it is a gift in the truest sense; I did nothing to earn or deserve it. But my faith in Jesus has never been moved, and I am consciously grateful for such a confidence.

I looked up at the people in the room in Lorna's home. They were all nodding knowingly at me and I really thought that this was perhaps an experience that everyone had - to sit in Jesus' lap, stand by a river. They seemed to know just what had happened.

I drove home full of more joy than I had ever had in my life. I sang at the top of my lungs every song I could think of from school choir that had anything about God in it. I knew I'd be in trouble for getting home late that night, but my heart was in another place entirely. I had compassion for my mother's concern. I allowed some understanding of why my father put rules in place. I'd accept my punishment quietly and let it go.

In an odd way, my new faith released me from my parents' wandering boundaries and ever-changing rules. My sister and I used to mock them in an attempt to make the craziness more palatable. We'd be in the middle of a game of Scrabble or gin rummy and one of us would look at the other and say, "New Rules!" and laugh at our in-joke. But now I knew ... well, I guess you could say it's like being Kosher; I had to answer to a higher authority.

I had to come home at times that were reasonable and safe, but I understood that my parents were broken. People have asked me whether the idea that everyone at Calvary Chapel called God "Our Father" was a problem for me. In fact, it was quite the opposite. I'd had a father who was a creep, so I needed a new one. It seemed like an easy switch from powerfully evil to powerfully good.

The next morning as I dressed for school I remembered a cross my half-sister had given me and retrieved it from the bottom of my closet. That was a tough one for me. Generally, I wore my peace symbol. Mind you, back then this was not simply a piece of jewelry one picked up at Sears. I say this because, years later, my daughter would bring home a pretty little silver one from the mall. I had to tell her that in my day, a peace symbol was made by hand, by an artisan, who lived in a little shack at the edge of town and wore sandals made of real tire treads. Mine was made of stained glass and hung around my neck with a leather cord. It meant a lot to me. I had to make a sort of inner choice that morning – to seek peace, but on my own terms, or to trust Someone else's terms for peace in my life. Self-consciously aware that no one in my life would guess I was a Christian, I put on the cross and headed for school.

# 6
# FOR THOSE TEARS I DIED

I was sort of nutty with joy that first day back at school. I was humming under my breath the only hymn I could remember that seemed relevant, "He arose, He arose, hallelujah, Christ arose!" over and over again. Everyone asked me what was up with me. I tried a hundred times to communicate, but "I got saved" or "I met Jesus" or "God is real and alive in my heart" just fell on incredulous ears.

Some people were openly argumentative, "Oh man, you sound like my grandma – don't be preaching at me." Others were dismissive, "Yeah, well whatever you're smoking, save me some." It seemed as though I had a hundred decisions to make. Oh, right, don't ditch class. Hmm, maybe I shouldn't lie to the teacher about my homework. Somehow, smoking in the girls' room before choir suddenly seemed a little disrespectful.

Choir had been a basic element to my survival of high school. The choir director, Sam Thompson, was open about being a Mormon. In those days, having high school choirs sing classical songs with Christian lyrics was commonplace, but Mr. Thompson picked some beautiful pieces. He had a sort of typical rhythm of discipline. He let us know how great choirs, or madrigals or other of the varied musical groups he organized were going to be – what competitions, field trips and tours we might take. Then he was very clear about the rules in the choir room. He said that he would kick anyone who broke them out of the group.

When the first person broke the rules, he kicked them out! I know it doesn't seem shocking, but we were not accustomed to adults actually doing that sort of thing. It had the effect of making us all pretty well behaved in choir. Mr. Thompson also came through on the trips and shows he had told us about during the year. He was an excellent director and several of his groups won competitions. We also put on a full production of a Broadway musical every year – and made money doing it because the shows were so popular with the local residents.

I think it had therefore mystified some people to know that Mr. Thompson allowed me to be in concert choir starting almost three years earlier in my freshman year. Even then, he had been protective of me. He did not allow me into the elite "madrigal" group, but he did allow me in concert choir early. He talked to me about my smoking, without ever asking me about it. That was actually pretty tricky. I no doubt would have lied about the blatant smell of tobacco smoke on my clothes and breath, but he never put me in that position. He connected me to an excellent vocal coach and simply told me how bad smoking was for my voice.

After my initial failure to positively convey my experience with Jesus to anyone at all that final week of my junior year in high school, I returned to the church at the beach the next Monday night. Although there was more of the building done, it was still only a wooden frame. I was so glad to be back where I could talk about what was going on in my heart. Pastor Chuck was doing a Bible study, but our interruptions didn't seem to faze him. In fact, he never seemed to mind when we butted in frequently to share a concern or ask a question.

I talked about how weird it was to find myself making good choices when nobody made me do it. I had awakened one morning during that first week and started to take my speed. No one had told me not to take it. People at Calvary Chapel at the time didn't preach "against" anything. They didn't tell us to stop taking drugs, dress more modestly, cut our hair, quit cussing…or be quiet in church. So I told them I was holding my drugs and found myself thinking *"I'll bet God could wake me up in the morning without my speed."* Trust me, I know this sounds unbearably naïve, but that was it. I really never took speed again. I never thought about it except to tell the other kids at church how weird it was.

Others shared similar experiences. Then one kid asked about demons. I was shocked, but then my whole worldview was shifting so I listened for the answer. Truthfully, when I thought of demons, I thought of my mother waking me from a dead sleep with her fingers curled like claws, screaming something unintelligible at me. To me that was the definition of "demonic;" seeing that my gentle, concerned mother had become that "other thing."

I waited for Pastor Chuck to give some long, adult, convoluted definition of demons. Instead he told us we didn't need to worry: Jesus had conquered hell and all that went with it, for us. All we had to do when we felt we encountered evil was to pray that it would be taken away, or driven out in Jesus' name. He read where Jesus had given His disciples that power, but he also made it sound so simple and reasonable.

I loved it. All week long when the evil in my home started up, I prayed to drive out the enemy and bind all evil in Jesus' name. As I write about it now, I think how "religious" that sounds to people who haven't heard things phrased that way, but at the time, I was just joyful to have some recourse.

A good example was the following week when Wendy came down the hall to my room. She was very upset, and no doubt highly skeptical of my newfound faith. She'd been to hell and back with me only a couple of years before and had seen me try on any number of beliefs. That night she wanted to talk about the times we had used the Ouija board to talk to spirits and how we'd gone to séances and had spirits talk to us. I think for her the showpieces of spiritualism– automatic handwriting or table lifting or spirits on the Ouija board - were at least evidence of something besides what we could see here.

I didn't want to tell her that I didn't believe that stuff anymore, so I tried reasonable logic. "Well why would we ask a spirit on the Ouija board what choices to make in our lives? How do we know who that spirit is – we wouldn't stop some stranger on the street and ask that, would we?" My questions and hers went on and on. The longer into the night we talked about this, the spookier everything got. We finally came to a point where we were so jumpy we felt like there were faces at the window. I thought I should try that "binding the enemy in Jesus' name" thing, but I felt this time I should not do that. The feelings continued to get more nightmarish. I thought, *"Well, I learned at church that sometimes God does things that don't make sense to us, so I'm going to go with my feeling and not do anything about it."* Wendy finally looked at me and started to cry. "This is so creepy. Can you make this stop?"

"Cool! Yes, I can," and prayed "that prayer". My sister gently opened her eyes again. "Hey, the room is lighter. Everything is gone."

I wanted so intensely for my sister to know that Jesus' love for her was real. We had lost ourselves in so many fantasies over the years – that *Twilight Zone* episode 'The Bewitching Pool' where the kids dive to the bottom of the pool to get away from their parents' fighting and swim up into a different world, which is magical like Wonderland or Neverland or Narnia. The fact that I knew Jesus now just seemed like another hopeless childhood wish to her.

The next week at the Bible study, I worried aloud that I may be "doing that prayer" too much. I didn't mean to be seeing a "demon" around every corner or blaming "the devil" for everything unpleasant that went on. But there seemed to be a lot of evil in my daily life. Pastor Chuck laughed. "You know," he said, "there's a story about a man who came to church and at testimony time every week, he'd start his story by saying, 'As I was walking along the path this week, I came against the enemy', and then he'd go on to tell a different event that he'd encountered."

"Finally", Chuck continued, "one of the other church members stood up and said, 'I'm just pretty tired of your stories over there, Brother. I walk along the path each week, and I never run into the enemy.' To which the first man shrugged, 'Maybe you're walkin' the same way he is.'"

That was really the basic message at Calvary Chapel back then. You can't do this wrong. There isn't a wrong way to pray. If you don't believe all that you should, the Holy Spirit will teach you what you need to know. If you're doing something that isn't pleasing to God, God will find a way to tell you. Read the Bible for yourself and ask Jesus to shed light on it for you. God knows your address, your name, your heart, as no one else ever can.

I think it was such a relief. It had not been hard for me to repent of my sins. I totally got it that anything that separated me from God was sin and I wasn't worried about superficial things or the guilt trips of my parents. I knew what lies and cruelties were found in their hearts. I was sorry for them. But now, Jesus inhabited my heart and I didn't have to be so scared anymore.

Pastor Chuck's example of why he didn't "preach against" anything at the time was that when one walked into a darkened room, it was ridiculous to try to get a baseball bat and drive all the darkness out. You just turned on the light. He talked about how a tiny match at the far corner of a dark room could be easily seen. He said there is really no such thing as "darkness." There is only lack of illumination. Light is the reality. You don't try to drive the darkness out; you just turn on the light!

I set about strategizing how in the world I could talk to my friends about Jesus. I thought about how much music and poetry had meant to me and how my first reaction when I felt the joy of the Lord was to sing every snippet of hymn or choir song about God I could remember. But I could hardly trot up to one of my friends and belt out the soprano line of a choir song. I thought about trying to write a song and realized I didn't even know if there were "rules" about songwriting. I mean, there were "rules" to haiku and sonnets and other forms of poetry.

So I grabbed a Peter, Paul and Mary record and played a song. I carefully wrote down how many syllables were in each line, how many lines in each verse and each chorus, which lines rhymed with others and how many times the chords changed. Then I closed my eyes and took myself back two weeks to that first moment with Jesus.

I didn't have my journal with me, so I tore open an envelope from a piece of junk mail. I wrote down what was important to me in those first moments, how everything had changed, how I sort of understood better when Jesus said He'd died to take away the tears of a broken-hearted child, how He'd been there every night, how humbled I was to see that I was special to Jesus.

I realized that the most important thing was that no matter what questions I ever had in my life, the answer was always going to be the same – come back to that first love. I had heard Him say stand by me at that river, there's always going to be enough water here to quench your thirst.

I got my guitar and I started to strum and write. It was a little hard because I was adhering strictly to the rhythm structure that I'd written down, but I was so sure of what I wanted to say. When I got to the chorus I knew with a deep peace that those words would be the answer to every question for the rest of my life. And, almost 50 years later, I realize that has been true.

When I was done, I sang it through twice. Then I decided I still might forget how it went, so I hauled out our big Wollensak reel-to-reel tape player. For those of you too young to remember those, they looked like gigantic cassette players (OK, so some of you don't remember those either), only the reel of tape on each side was separate and about 7 inches in diameter, so you had to take out the machine and thread the tape from one reel to the other through the recording part.

I managed to remember the song long enough to get all of that set up, and I recorded *For Those Tears I Died.* I titled it that because that part was so important to me, but everyone else called it *"Come to the Water."*

*For Those Tears I Died* (*Come to the Water*)- Marsha Stevens
*copyright EMI 1969*

*You said You'd come and share all my sorrows,*
*You said You'd be there for all my tomorrows,*
*I came so close to sending You away,*

*But just like You promised, You came there to stay,*
*I just had to pray.*

*CHORUS:*
*And Jesus said, "Come to the water, stand by my side,*
*I know you are thirsty, you won't be denied.*
*I felt every teardrop when in darkness you cried,*
*And I strove to remind you, that for those tears I died."*

*Your goodness so great, I can't understand,*
*And, dear Lord, I know that all this was planned.*
*I know You're here now and always will be,*
*Your love loosed my chains and in You I'm free,*
*But Jesus why me? (back to chorus)*

*Jesus, I give You my heart and my soul,*
*I know that without God I'd never be whole,*
*Savior, You opened all the right doors,*
*And I thank You and praise You from earth's humble shores,*
*Take me I'm Yours.*

# 7
## PERFORMING MY FIRST SONG

After packing the Wollensak away, I went running upstairs to find my sister when I remembered Wendy was next door at her friend's house. Her friend was a teacher and a sort of mentor to her, and I had little doubt that she was over there talking about me and how I'd lost my mind. It was one thing to play with spooky board games, but it was another entirely to believe in Jesus.

To me it was like Dorothy finding out that all her answers were in her own back yard, but for my sister, it was as though I suddenly thought the Wizard of Oz was the fountain of all truth. I bumbled in with my guitar and said triumphantly, "I wrote a song!" They both sat back patiently to listen.

My sister told me later that when I started to sing, "You said You'd come and share all my sorrows, You said You'd be there for all my tomorrows," she thought to herself, "Oh hurray. Marsha finally has a boyfriend." Then when I got to, "I just had to pray," she felt embarrassed that I was singing a *religious* song in front of her friend.

But by the end of the song, they were both crying and I felt exultant that they "got it" at last. I threw my guitar over my back and sang the song to a couple more friends and by the next Monday night, on our hour drive to Bible study at Calvary Chapel, my sister had worked out a harmony to sing with me.

We brought along another friend that night, one who would become an important part of our lives and music. Pete Jacobs had sometimes crashed at our house. His mother had mental problems and had kicked him out of his house or made him stay on a cot in a sort of small wash shack behind the house. It didn't have a bathroom or place for him to shower, and of course, no refrigerator, so we'd let him stay over.

Pete was an odd arrangement of geek and cool. He wasn't classically handsome, but he had perpetually smiling eyes. He didn't fit neatly into any of the generally recognized categories of teenage cliques at the time. He wasn't a jock or a hippie. He didn't do drugs. Mostly, he was a phenomenal jazz musician. When the high school concert choir sang at other community venues, part of the show was for the choir director to ask anyone in the crowd to play any piece of music on any instrument and Pete would come up and play it right after them.

People heard about the challenge and someone would come to play *"Flight of the Bumblebee"* (Rimsky-Korsakov) on the piano or bring their French horn, tuba, flute, trombone, oboe, and on and on. Pete played each piece on whatever instrument they brought. His was an extraordinary musical gift.

He had entered his jazz quartet into the Hollywood Bowl Battle of the Bands in the Jazz Division and won that year after the band not only played spectacularly, but did it while passing four different instruments around and around among three players, like a game of musical chairs (the drummer stayed on drums).

Pete had a soft heart and listening ear and would scrape together his last dollar to treat a hurting friend to an ice cream at the local Betsy Ross Ice Cream Parlor. Although he and I had flirted on and off, I realized he actually felt like an adopted brother to me. We had both attended a fairly secular church together from time to time in previous years.

At that church there had been a coffeehouse called "Agape" and I would find out much later that this was a Greek word for unconditional love, like the love of God for people. It is funny now, but at the time we thought it was an Indian word that meant "free love." That church coffeehouse was raided one night and 20 drug arrests were made. So we thought it was a cool place to hang out and expand our minds. Now, I was terribly anxious for Pete to find his own relationship with Jesus.

As we headed to Calvary Chapel the next Monday night, Pete was thoroughly skeptical and was watching Wendy like a hawk to see if this was just something I was going to coerce her into tonight. I was actually pretty nervous about singing again at Calvary Chapel. Remember the only time I'd sung before; they hadn't been thrilled with my choice of song. I was ready for Lonnie Frisbee to stand up after my song this time and say, "Jesus didn't say, "Come to the water, He said come unto me," or correct some other doctrinal failure on my part.

I brought in my guitar, introduced my kid sister again, since the group had grown so much in just a few weeks. Together, we sang my song. And it was more than I hoped for. I have to say that for someone who thought I was caught up in a "trip," my sister made up the most beautiful, creative harmony to the song. When we finished Pastor Chuck had tears in his eyes. Others were crying openly. People were mostly just silent for a few seconds. Then Lonnie stood up and said, "That's from the book of Revelation, chapter 21, verse 6."

I was overjoyed. I was only halfway through Matthew and God had told me something from the very end of the book!

Chuck went on with the Bible study and we all went to Lorna and Bill's again afterward. People were talking, singing songs ("He's the Savior of My Soul") and somewhere in the middle of it all, my little sister knelt down to pray. I wanted to chatter all the way home, but Wendy was very quiet. Where I had been singing at the top of my lungs, she was all too silent and Pete was scrutinizing her. I had to make them both talk a little bit - I had to stay awake and drive.

Pete watched Wendy in the days that followed and saw the utter transformation in her. He came the next week and stayed to meet Jesus, too. His experience was different in his own way. He didn't feel the sudden change that Wendy and I did, but when he woke up the next morning he realized he was opening his eyes to a new life. Every thought and perspective and sound was new. Pete would be a big part of our musical ministry from then on.

I found Dale, who had saved me from my suicide plan just two years earlier and sang my song for her. Now all of us were talking to friends and our one car was packed. There were no seat belt laws then; it was the era of 'how-many-people-can-you-fit-into-your-Volkswagen?' Ours was overflowing with kids.

One of those teenagers was Russ Stevens, who played in Pete's band. He was not just the bass player in the band, but played several instruments himself as well. Russ was definitely further along the geek scale from Pete. He was a good kid from a kind family without hidden cruelties or addictions. He wore black horned-rim glasses that almost hid soft brown eyes. His "conversion experience" was more cerebral than mine. He had more of a feeling that "this" made sense of everything. I had no idea yet that Russ would be my future husband.

One Monday night we found ourselves lacking guitars, and a piano had not yet been installed in the church. We realized we could sing acapella (sans instruments and with harmony). I was a soprano, Wendy an alto, Russ a tenor and Pete a bass. That meant we could sing one of those cool choir songs I had sung on my first ride home with Jesus.

Pete had perfect pitch, so he gave us our notes and we launched into *"At the Round Earth's Imagined Corners."* This was John Donne's poem set to music by Williametta Spencer. For weeks after that we would have fun singing choir songs to a bunch of new hippie Christians.

There's a YouTube video of us singing Bach's *"All Breathing Life."* Pete could start us and keep us in the right key, Russ had a soaring tenor and while Wendy's voice was softer than mine, her pitch was better. She could sing any sequence of notes to make the harmonies work. I thought that was probably the most fun we had during all our years of singing together. We'd be sitting in a Denny's restaurant and just launch into *"The Hallelujah Chorus"* at the drop of a hat.

Baptism

On another Monday night at the Bible study, someone asked Pastor Chuck if we shouldn't be baptized. He agreed, but everything about us was so unconventional. How could we do it? He asked, "If we tried to end a bit early next Monday night, would some of you like to stay afterward since school is out now? We could all go down to the 19th street bay at Newport Beach. Bring a towel and a change of clothes."

Few of us had ever seen a baptism other than a few drops on a newborn's head, but we did as we were told. I was so excited. My half-sister, Kay, heard me say I wanted to be baptized. My half-brother Charles came to cheer me on, and of course Wendy and Pete were there. It would actually have been a great time to invite my parents, who thought there must be something completely clandestine going on with all those hippies at the church, but it never occurred to me to ask them.

There ended up being a bigger group than I had anticipated although it was dark and you couldn't see anything in front of you. This was before we started doing huge daytime Saturday baptisms at Corona del Mar. On this night we got quiet as Chuck explained that this was an important moment in our lives in Christ. He told us that baptism meant we'd be leaving our old selves buried in the water at the 19th street bay and come up out of the water as new "creatures in Christ." We were making a public stand, aligning ourselves as followers of Jesus.

I remember praying with Pastor Chuck and realizing that I trusted his strong arms and sure experience to be certain I wouldn't drown. I came up out of the water, exuberant, to find that everyone had learned the chorus to my first song, so they could surprise me by singing my words, "And Jesus said, 'Come to the water...'". I was sobbing and laughing. It was the first time anyone else had sung one of my songs. It was also the first time a newspaper sent a photographer to see what was going on with all these hippie kids on Monday nights. The big flashbulb popped right in front of me as

I waded out of the water into the arms and towels of my sisters and brothers in Christ.

I stayed in the Bluebird motel where Lonnie and his wife, Connie, were staying that summer. We read the Bible endlessly. Lonnie was a patient teacher who would give you the answers to questions that made Pastor Chuck squirm a bit. If you wanted to know why someone thought the Bible said not to sleep with your girlfriend before you got married, Lonnie would look up Scriptures with you about commitments and promises, and what it means for your body to be a temple of the Holy Spirit. He would talk specifically with you about "how far was too far," and so on. Chuck would give us the old adage about how 'a woman gives sex to get love and a man gives love to get sex.' That made men sound awfully creepy, I thought.

Anyway, the next hurdle I found myself face to face with was going back to summer camp with Audrey. This was back in the days before the Internet, when your parents rarely allowed long distance calls even to family, let alone to a friend from camp. Audrey and I wrote letters to each other, but I hadn't written to her before camp. I called her as the week approached and in a very short phone call, I said, "There's some REALLY important stuff we're going to have to talk about the FIRST night at camp."

She said, "Yeah there's stuff I need to tell you about too. But you know what. I heard a song I think you might like to learn how to play," and in her sweet variable pitch, she started to sing,
"And Jesus said, 'Come to the water, stand by my side...'"
I was speechless. "Where did you hear that song???"
"A friend of mine heard it somewhere and taught it to us."

At the time, I only thought about how cool it was of Jesus to let Audrey and me learn about Him at the same time. But it was the beginning of a song that was written on the hearts of the Jesus Movement. There was no advertising campaign. No radio stations were playing that kind of music. No recording companies were offering contracts. It just went from person to person and heart to heart. It was one of the joys of the early Jesus Music that there was no ulterior motive for writing a song or singing in a band. The only reason to do it was to share your love for Jesus with a friend.

Audrey and I went to at least 3 weeks of camp that summer at Pilgrim Pines, the United Church of Christ youth camp. We cringed later to remember how self-righteous and clique-ish we were with our newfound faith. Once when we walked out to the porch of the cabin where we stayed, our counselor asked if we were leaving. We turned to her and said, "You would know if we were leaving because we would have our Bibles with us." And, in fact, we did carry them everywhere. I had a better concordance than Audrey did and we used it many times a day. A concordance is an alphabetical list of keywords in the Bible, which then refers you to where those words are found. This was long before search engines or the Internet.

So if another camper asked us a question, we would industriously go through the concordance to see if we could find the answer for them. I think by the end of the summer camp season we had become a bit humbler and at least more approachable. I sang *"For Those Tears I Died"* and it was in the camp's sing-along book by the next summer. I guess they must have survived our youthful arrogance.

By the end of summer 1969, the church building at Calvary Chapel was finished and the carpeting and pews went in. I was walking in barefoot one Sunday morning with friends when Tony, the usher, stopped me. "You know, you kids can't be coming in barefoot like this anymore. You're bringing in sand that'll ruin the new shag carpets."

We weren't offended. We ran back out to see how many pairs of flip-flops we could find in our car trunks. At the end of the church service, Pastor Chuck quietly said, "After this last hymn, I'd like everyone to stay in your seats for a brief congregational meeting." After the benediction he said, "We need volunteers to stay after service to tear out the new carpeting." That startled everyone. There were various protestations and questions called out. Pastor Chuck said, "I heard these kids were told that they couldn't come in barefoot from the beach anymore. No one will be turned away from this church. If that means tearing out the carpets, then we'll do that today." He paused. "And if the studs on their blue jeans scratch the pews, we'll tear them out, too."

The carpets and pews stayed in, and so did we; bare feet, blue jeans and all.

Way too soon, school started again. It was my senior year. The new high school choir director asked me if I had copyrighted the songs I was writing. I thought that was the silliest thing I'd ever heard. Who was going to swipe my songs? Who cared? But Mr. Caton made it a graded assignment for me to copyright my songs. I remember being glad as I struggled to write the music down note by note that so much of the verse was on the same note. When I met Mr. Caton again, 15 years later at Metropolitan Community Church of San Diego, I remembered to thank him for that advice so many years before.

Although several kids had come to Calvary Chapel with me over the summer, a few were a year ahead of me and had already graduated. Many were in my sister's class three years behind me. Several were in Russ or Pete's group of friends who were basically known as "good kids" already. I was by far the most visibly different person and I took endless teasing about it. Being off speed and having quit smoking, I had started to gain weight. I had a friend ask me if I was going to get over Christianity before I exploded. But most of the teasing came with questions and I was deeply aware of the searching hearts around me.

Some of the friends we spoke to went to Claremont Theological Seminary to ask about this new "Jesus Movement." The counselors they spoke to were disparaging of our "religious malarkey" and warned them to stay away from this crazy belief system. I have no doubt the counselors believed there was some secondary motive going on to get just one more dollar in the plate or to tell kids they were going to hell. As a matter of fact, no offering plates were ever passed at the services we attended and the idea of giving any "negative" theology was actively discouraged.

Besides that, outside our little community of Jesus people, this was not the season of church and innocence as we closed out the 1960's. It was the time of civil rights marches for African-Americans and Latino/Latina itinerant workers. It was a time of protesting the Vietnam war, draft dodging and bra burning. Haight/Ashbury was the crossroads for all the "don't trust anyone over 30" crowd, and the murders organized by Charles Manson took place. Medgar Evers, a civil rights activist had been murdered in Mississippi earlier in the decade, and that had caused his family to move far away. They came to Claremont. The slain man's daughter went to high school with me. It was not the time to be religious and I knew it

The worst mockers were my own teachers. After Alisa, who was now the editor of the school newspaper, published an article about me called "What's up with All This Jesus Jazz?" the teasing just didn't quit. The article was published early in my senior year. It was serious and well written, but the notoriety was not always fun. One day, on my way to class, a student I'll call Della stopped me to ask me if I could pray with her. I was stunned. Della was always dressed in black, a loner who let no one close. She told me her father was abusing her and she didn't know how to get help, that she thought she was a bad person. I did all I could to pray with her and assure her that we'd find some way to get help and that God adored her, and then ran into class.

The teacher said, "Why are you late, Marsha?" I apologized, climbing into my seat, and said I'd stay to talk afterward and explain. But he didn't want to let up. "Oh come on, Marsha," he said sarcastically. "I think we all want to know why a *Christian* would be tardy."

I said, "I stopped to pray with someone."
"Oh right, no doubt." He retorted. Several in the class snickered.

Another time a student asked about the "truth" of what was written in our history books. The teacher jumped up to start a conversation about "truth," but stopped first to say, "That's a great question: What is truth? And Marsha, why don't you do us all a favor and stay out of it."

I was reading the New Testament and there were lots of people who were derided, mocked, and martyred. I thought I was getting off pretty easy in that regard. The dean of girls asked me into her office. This was the same dean of girls who had tried to talk to me about my suicide plans and had engineered a way for me to get a pregnancy test just a year before. She asked me what had been said in my various classes and I told her. I also told her I felt badly. I wasn't mad. I knew they just "didn't get me." She said that was still inappropriate and that the school had decided to "give my side equal time."

This "equal time" thing was a big deal in the 60's. Even radio and TV stations which were determined to have given one side of an issue airtime, were required to give the other side "equal time." Actually, that was not technically the Equal Time law, but it was in the spirit of the Fairness Doctrine which was in place from shortly after the end of World War II to 1987.

I decided to go for broke and ask if my pastor could come to the classes where teachers had openly disparaged me. You probably want to note that it never occurred to me what an imposition that might be on the pastor of a growing church to drive an hour each way to speak in high school history and social studies classes. I did wonder if he'd send Lonnie Frisbee, the consummate hippie. People would tell Lonnie that with his long hair and sandals that he looked like Jesus.

But it was Pastor Chuck who came. I could see that it was unnerving for some of my classmates to have such a normal-seeming guy actually turn out to be "that preacher from the hippie church." Chuck didn't pontificate. He listened to questions about why bad things happen to good people. He addressed the question of how it could be that Christianity was true or how we could ever KNOW it was true. What happens to babies in Africa who never even had the chance to "become Christians?"

He flipped through Scriptures about bad things that happened in the Bible and what ultimately resulted in the lives of those who experienced them. He comforted kids who were in the middle of some pain themselves. He talked about how Christianity was a "faith" rather than an area of study and how at some point you'd just have to take that leap and see for yourself if someone was really there. He assured them that God's love and concern for everyone was certain, so unless one of us was deciding whether to enter a mission field we'd just have to trust that God's plan included everyone. He read from the Bible about assurances we could have concerning each of these things. The teacher was almost apoplectic and I thought he might leave the room.

Then Chuck asked if there was anyone in the room besides me who considered themselves a Christian. "I mean a Christian in your own right, and not just by the beliefs of your parents." I was stunned to see a few other kids in the class raise their hands. One guy sat right next to me. I thought, *"How did you sit there and watch what was happening to me in that class on an almost daily basis, and never stick up for me?"* I tried to understand what it might be like to consider Jesus a "gimme" in life, to take the Christian faith for granted without thought.

That day became a turning point for me in how I understood what it meant to stand up for Jesus. I never wanted to be silent when someone else was struggling to be true to themselves. The year was filled with countless Monday night trips to Calvary Chapel. There were growing numbers of kids believing that Jesus could and would change their lives and give them purpose, and would keep them safe in His own heart.

One of the times that thought stuck with me was a music practice at school. I think it might have been an evening practice, but in any case, Russ Stevens and I were doing more than making music these days. We were flirting, but kind of like little kids. We were throwing papers at each other, and stealing each other's sheet music. Then Russ grabbed my sheet music and dashed through one of those big steel doors they have in schools. Barefoot, as usual, I got my foot in the door just as it closed. I broke two toes and one was really just dangling with blood pouring out of it. I moved back stunned, as the blood pooled around my foot. Russ immediately grabbed towels and started to pray for the bleeding to stop, which it did.

Then we all waited for the choir director to show up so that someone would be the grown up and tell us what to do. Another student called my parents from the school phone and started with that second-worst-of-all opening to a phone call, "Marsha's fine, but..." Then I started to sing one of our choir songs: Hall Johnson's, *"Lord, I keep so busy praisin' my Jesus, keep so busy praisin' my Jesus, keep so busy praisin' my Jesus, Ain't got time to die."* It took my mind off the pain.

Russ helped me sing my way through the next few hours. The doc in the ER sewed my toes back together and put me on crutches. I spent the next two agonizing weeks learning what it means that when the smallest part of the body suffers, the WHOLE body suffers!

The final shock of my senior year of high school was the Senior Awards at the very end of the school year. I had no intention of going to the awards. I didn't have the highest grades or the best SAT's. I wasn't the prom queen or head cheerleader. I wasn't on the girls' softball team, and more importantly, I wasn't even a Girl Scout or community leader and those who were had always won something. But everyone kept urging me to go. I tried to think of what friend of mine might be winning something that made people want me to come. I have always disliked contests and labeling who is "best" and who didn't quite measure up. I hate to lose but I don't like to "beat" anyone else either, so I avoid those situations.

Reluctantly, I showed up, advertising my discomfort with the whole ordeal by wearing an old homemade granny dress with a stain on it and sitting in the back row, barefoot again. The music awards went by without me hearing any friends' names called. I was about to leave when they announced The Christian Service Award and called my name.

I cannot begin to tell you the ways I was stunned. For one thing, I had Jewish friends and I had been almost certain that the school called this The Community Service Award. Then I thought about the girl who had won it the year before. Faith was a tall, slender, very proper girl who sat beside me in choir. She was brilliant, responsible, the recipient of the Bank of America scholarship and numerous community activity awards. She was active in Girl Scouts, and was the cooking, housekeeping, table-setting, winning awards kind at the Los Angeles county fair. She was most definitely NOT an overweight, barefoot hippie in a granny dress. Who on earth decided these awards? I wasn't aware any adults even liked me. Clearly, since I remember it so vividly over 40 years later, it meant a lot to me.

# 8
# 'CHILDREN OF THE DAY' IS BORN

As I continued to read the Bible and share it, I frequently received disrespectful comments. A lot of people were treated badly over sharing the ways of God. I actually considered it sort of pro forma – to be expected. But we started being questioned in another way: why did we all drive an hour to church at least once a week? This was something that adults especially questioned. We honestly wondered about it, too. Why weren't there other churches we could find that allowed teenagers to come even if their parents did not attend? Were there leaders who talked normally on the church platform, not like some crazy hyped up performer, or an elderly orator? We didn't know the answer ourselves, but we tried to find out.

Pete and I went to every different church we knew of, and sometimes Wendy or Russ joined with us. We went to the Catholic Church and asked them why they prayed to 'idols' in the church (statues) and why people called the priest "Father". They explained that it was no different than asking a friend to pray for you, and that "Father" was a term of respect.

We went to a liberal Jewish congregation and to a conservative Jewish temple and asked both of them why they didn't believe Jesus was actually the Messiah. We asked what they did believe about the Messiah, and they patiently showed us their Scripture and what it meant to them. We went to the United Church of Christ with the coffee house and asked why they seemed to only teach that Jesus was a good teacher and a nice man – just like a million other nice guys. We visited the Jehovah's Witnesses and asked why they wouldn't take blood transfusions. We visited the Seventh Day Adventists and asked why they didn't meet on Sunday and then to the Mormons to see why they believed they'd be in a higher place in heaven than the rest of us. We asked why they believed in "eternal marriage" when Jesus said it wasn't like that in heaven. Most importantly, we listened to the answers. We were never there to argue. We really wanted to know – and there were some good answers.

The Mormon kids pounced right back. They wanted to tell us ALL about the Latter Day Saints and we sat around with them for hours talking about the Bible and Book of Mormon. Finally, they asked us to come to some kind of service they were having. We tried to make them a deal – we'd go to theirs and then they'd come to ours. They stunned us by saying they weren't allowed to do that. They challenged us to ask our pastor if we'd be "allowed" to come to their church. We felt almost ridiculous doing that, but the next Monday night we did. We told everyone where all we'd been and what various people had told us and waited for a reaction from Lonnie or Pastor Chuck.

Chuck immediately lit up, "That's great guys. Good job. You're being just like the Bereans who Paul wrote about in Acts 17. It says they received the Word but then searched the scriptures themselves to 'see if things were so' or to see if they were true." We told him about our deal to go to the Mormons service if they'd come to ours. He said that'd be great. "Go wherever you feel led to go. You know we'd welcome them here any time."

I have to say that all these things were a wonderful gift in laying the foundation of my faith. Calvary Chapel was not dense with doctrine then, we trusted the Holy Spirit to "lead us into all truth." I understood already that defending your faith or explaining it to others was never going to be an easy thing. I think I had it much better than kids for whom Christianity was a given in their lives. They were the kids who went to church and expected everyone to think of them as good; who accepted the faith of their parents without questions of their own. My whole foundation in Christ was about studying the Word, and about sharing what Jesus was doing in my life.

It was about "working out my own salvation." Chuck would point out that people stopped too soon in reading that scripture, because it goes on to say, "work out your own salvation with fear and trembling for *it is God at work in you* both to will and to do His good pleasure." Philippians 2:12 KJV. Calvary Chapel was not involved in politics at that time either. It was just a place where everyone was welcome, whether or not we ruined the rugs. We were loved and accepted just as we were.

The school talent show was just a couple of weeks before school ended. The four of us – Wendy, Russ, Pete and I – sang *For Those Tears I Died*, along with some other folk songs. By that time a couple of other churches in the area had asked me to talk, and to sing that song to their youth groups. Summer camps put it in their songbooks.

One afternoon a friend called me to say they were coming to hear me speak at a local Four Square church. I asked what they were talking about and they said it was in the paper. I picked out the Religious Section and saw with mild horror that it called me a promiscuous young hippie drug user who had gotten saved and that I would be speaking at their church Sunday night. I was used to singing, but not sharing my story in public.

Remember that I had just turned 17 and was not at all good at setting boundaries. I phoned the church number and the pastor breezily told me that he thought someone had confirmed it with me. After my father's notoriety in the local paper I did know that many people would actually read that page. I had to find a way to give a quick run-down to my parents. They knew, of course, about my conversion, but trying to cover free love, the extent of which was sleeping with the boyfriend who lived 2 ½ hours away, and "turn on/ tune in/drop out" ways of living was awkward.

My father pretty much acted as though he had known all along. My mother sobbed hysterically. We knew some of the disasters in my half-brother's life that had resulted from him taking drugs. She asked me, "How could you ever take drugs when you knew how badly they affected your brother?" I found that sort of a weird question. I reminded her of all the stories we've heard about drinking alcohol and about the aunt on my father's side who had died looking 9 months pregnant with cirrhosis of the liver. "But you still drink." I responded.

I hated those kinds of interactions with my Mom. At the time, I didn't know the root cause of her starting on alcohol. She didn't tell me about her teen years with my father until after he passed away. But I could always verbally get the best of her in an argument. The problem was that it didn't make me feel best. It only made both of us feel worse. I felt more distant from her, and she felt overwhelming shame at her mistakes.

I did speak, as announced, at the Foursquare Church that Sunday night. I think they were expecting me to be a little "better witness" of Christ's changes in my life. They did not expect a heavy-set, tie-dyed, barefoot hippie to be sharing from their pulpit. They thought I would have known at least how to dress for church. Of course, this was exactly how I dressed for church.

One day, the phone rang at my house and it was Pat Boone. He was asking if he could perform and record my song, "For Those Tears I Died." I had a vague idea who he was – I remembered the short movie rom my first night at Calvary Chapel. I knew he sang for my mother's generation and wore white shoes. That was about it. I found the question startling, though, and had a fleeting desire to be flippant like my mother and say, "I don't know, can you?"

It felt to me like calling an author and saying, "Can I read your book?" But I told him, sure. That was totally fine. I didn't mind at all. I have found, since then, that this is not always true for other songwriters, and it was very gracious of Pat to call me and ask. Over the years I've heard beautiful songs that the composers did not want sung, usually because they were certain they would be "discovered" and someone more famous would sing it.

But for us, there were only a handful of groups even trying to write "Jesus Music" and there was no one to discover any of us. I did fervently hope that he would not have dancing girls in go go boots singing the harmonies to my music, though! Ultimately, he recorded two of my songs and I was honored that he did. As of this writing, you can hear Pat singing *"For Those Tears I Died"* on YouTube: https://www.youtube.com/watch?v=yKpqazwPUns

One Monday night, we had brought some really emotionally hurting friends to church. They stayed afterward, wanting to talk to someone about getting to know Jesus. We heard a phone ringing in the office and someone came out and got Wendy and me to respond to the call. It was a family friend calling to tell us that our mother had been hurt in a car accident. She had already been drinking when she drove to the corner liquor store to buy more alcohol. She was in an accident on the way home. She'd been taken to the hospital for sutures and was released. The police knew my father who passed it off to "having one too many," and they let him take her home and take care of the accident. Our quandary was that we had friends we had brought all this way to hear about Jesus. But now that our mother was hurt, I was deeply conflicted.

I knew the Bible said to honor your father and mother, so I asked Pastor Chuck. He had picked up a lot of the backstory of our lives from the things we'd shared in church. I told him what had happened and asked what I should do. He shook his head and looked down and it seemed to me like he felt the burden of our everyday lives for a moment. He said, "Marsha, there's nothing that you can do for your mother. She's home now and safe. You have a responsibility to God to take care of yourselves, too. The Bible does say to honor your mother and father and I believe you do that. You don't sass them anymore or cause them needless worry. But Jesus also said that anyone who has given up houses or lands, or father, or mother and so on for my name's sake will receive back a hundredfold. If you stay tonight, just be sure you are staying for HIS name's sake."

I felt liberated. The situation at home had gotten so bad that Wendy and I, and often our friend Pete, felt as though we were completely on our own in the world. We stayed that night, and our friends gave their hearts to Jesus. My father berated us when we got home, but it didn't diminish our joy for our friends. I asked Chuck if we could call him Papa Chuck. I have done so ever since that night.

We decided to perform at more concerts and called ourselves Children of the Day. We loved that Scripture from First Thessalonians 5:5 KJV, "You are all the children of light and the children of the day, not of the darkness."

Pete set about to try to make some kind of musicians of Wendy and me. He wrote more songs with Wendy and me as lead vocalists. We began to apply for college scholarships and we had an interesting experience when we went to audition at Azusa Pacific College. We were too young and naïve to think that anyone might know about the Jesus Movement yet. People had only recently begun calling it that in the media. We were more concerned that our obvious lack of sophistication would disqualify us. Russ had to tell me that shoes were an absolute requirement.

We brought our guitars and I think Russ may have brought his stand-up bass, and prepared two songs. The people for whom we performed, all older white men, introduced themselves, but not their positions at the college. We just sang for one guy after another. We were a little concerned that we were being passed on so many times. One man tried to have Pete teach us a different cutesy ending for his song "New Life." That surprised me. Not only was it a completely odd and old-fashioned ending, but...it wasn't his song. It was Pete's. I hadn't run into that kind of presumptuousness before. With all the "kids" at Calvary Chapel, Pastor Chuck and other leaders had always treated us with welcome and respect for the gifts and talents and new perspectives we brought.

At Azusa Pacific scholarship auditions, we were ultimately sent to the office of an even older, white-haired gentleman, who scowled disapprovingly at our guitars and stopped us halfway through our first song with a raised hand. "We don't sing that sort of... *stuff* in Concert Choir," he stated in a flat tone and turned in his chair to dismiss us. "Oh," said Pete, "We didn't know you were the choir director. Umm, do you have a piano nearby? We could sing the trio from the Saint Saens Christmas Oratorio."

Furry eyebrows rose at least an inch into his forehead, but Professor Anderson led us into the next room. At the time, I could still sing the interval from the G above middle C to a high B-flat that occurs in that trio. We could see we had confounded him. 'Prof,' as everyone would call him for the next several years, began a series of questions. Most of them were musical and were therefore fielded by Russ and Pete. Prof eyed Wendy curiously but then asked to hear our other songs after all. He asked if I had written *"For Those Tears I Died"* and why. Then he began to tell us how hard we would have to work in choir this year if we were going to get ready for our tour of Europe and Israel the next summer. They offered the three of us half of their entire music scholarship budget for freshmen that year and we got ready to go to college. We were ecstatic!

We had all dated one another on and off my senior year and the following summer. Wendy had actually dated Russ before I did. I had begun to assume that in one combination or another, we would eventually marry. But our consuming passion was music and sharing Jesus. Pete and I butted heads a lot but we loved each other a lot, too. Of the four of us, we were the two who wore our hearts on our shirtsleeves. But I admired Russ' quiet demeanor, his self-confidence. Unlike Pete, Russ had only spent one night at the big Claremont house where Wendy and I lived. He never forgot the intensity of conflict between my parents. I didn't even realize it was a particularly bad night. There was some shouting and scuffles between my parents and I was a bit embarrassed, but Russ was horrified.

The next morning he was visibly shaken and said he would never again spend the night at that house. I kind of loved that. He told me he had never heard his parents fight. I also knew that both he and Pete had given up more impressive colleges to come to Azusa Pacific College where we could attend together and continue to sing as a group, and I appreciated that about both of them.

Pete and I taught summer Sunday school classes at our old church, all of us were at Calvary Chapel for every Bible study we could get to, and then college hit. I think all four of us were a little surprised at just how much the college wanted us to do for our scholarships. They began booking Children of the Day at least 4 to 7 times a week. Sometimes it was for a short appearance at a Wednesday night youth group meeting in the local area for just a song or two. Other times they wanted us to do a set of songs when the Concert Choir or other college music groups were performing, and we would be the sort of intermission group. And of course some were full concerts at churches and community events.

They could also book us on Sunday mornings since Pete played piano and we did not require our guitars, which were still not allowed in hardly ANY church's morning service. It seems funny looking back that only certain instruments were considered church-appropriate.

There were many Sundays the college had us doing a song at a pre-service Bible Study at one church, two songs for special music at a worship service at another church, a concert in a park or other outdoor venue in the afternoon, and a mini-concert at a youth group meeting at a 3rd church on Sunday night. It was our baptism by fire into the world of performing music.

Saturdays were similarly booked as were several weeknights. Russ was the first one to express concern about how we needed time to do homework. Pete and I had taken mostly music and Bible classes, and I had an honors English class, so most of those were no-brainers for us. On our most overbooked week, we calculated that we had sung 14 times from Sunday to Sunday. This was preparing us for what was coming next.

# 9
# OUR FIRST ALBUM

In 1970 we decided we wanted to record an album. Pete and Russ had done one for the PJQ (Pete Jacob's Quartet), so they had some experience. There was no record company remotely interested in Jesus Music yet, so we had to figure it out ourselves. Papa Chuck loaned us $1,000 and we went to a studio in Hollywood where we met Buck Herring. Buck was very supportive of us. He played a recording he had made of his wife, along with her brother and sister. Buck's wife Annie had a great voice, but Buck was frustrated with the recording industry. Some pop groups had come out with some fairly innocuous "Put Your Hand in the Hand" type songs. But Buck said, "My wife, and her brother Matt and sister Nelly want to make a recording too, but we just won't do what they want us to do. The big record companies don't want us to be too direct about putting faith in Christ. They want us to be hip and cool, but if I want to say, 'Give your heart to Jesus,' I most certainly am not going to say, 'Hand your pump to The Man upstairs.'

Buck introduced us to the need to be ready to record. In the studio, the clock was running. We went to his house to rehearse sometimes since he lived close to the studio. His wife, Annie, had the most precious habit of popping in and out of prayer all the time, as though Jesus was right there, part of every conversation. I almost expected her to ask Jesus to pass the peas.

I related well to her and her kid sister, Nellie. Wendy was with us at recording sessions, so she talked little sister stuff with Nellie, while Annie and I spoke as big sisters. Their folks had died, so Annie's younger sister and brother had both moved in with them. I understood taking care of your sister like that.

Her brother, Matt Ward, was harder to get to know. Annie said he was shy because his voice was changing and I heard it crack once or twice. The thing was that it was very important for him to sing with his sisters, so he would disappear into the basement and practice vocalizing for hours like someone training for an Olympic event. You could tell that, of course, once they began to tour as the very successful Christian group, "The Second Chapter of Acts," and record for themselves.

Many times Matt was said to have the most talented and instantly recognizable male voice in Contemporary Christian Music. We listened back then to Annie as she sat at the piano and had songs just flow out of her. I was fascinated by all the rules she broke; there were songs with no chorus at all or where the verses each had a different number of lines in them. That didn't bother her in the least and she wrote some of the most creative and best-loved songs of the Jesus Movement – all without ever once having to say, "Hand your pump to The Man Upstairs."

We had friends from college play different instruments on our album. Wendy made her first contribution to our song writing with "As a Child". It's hard to remember just how much that was true for her. She was only 14 years old when we first started playing as Children of the Day.

After talking to Annie about taking care of kid sisters, I spoke to my dorm mother at Azusa. She allowed Wendy to stay in my room as long as there were no complaints. Claremont High School, which even then was very progressive for its day, allowed Wendy to take some college courses and transfer them for high school credits. Azusa Pacific College was fine with that process as well.

Calvary Chapel decided since no one else seemed to want to record any Jesus Music, they would do it themselves. Calvary Chapel incorporated Maranatha! Music, with one of Chuck Smith's relatives at the helm. They made a group album that included Children of the Day and they called it *"The Everlastin' Living Jesus Music Concert."* Immediately after that, they released the Children of the Day's first album, *"Come to the Water."*

By then other groups, like Love Song, Gentle Faith, Blessed Hope, Debbie Kerner and several others were ready to record. This was the beginning of amazing ministry opportunities and outreach beyond all we could have imagined. This was also the beginning of putting tender eager new Christians in the middle of what would become a billion-dollar industry.

# 10
# BALANCING CONCERTS AND COLLEGE

Back at college, we were worrying about classes, papers and finals, as well as getting ready for our summer tour. Pete sailed through his music classes, much to the dismay of instructors who wanted him to be more humble in his learning process. Russ was the best at studying and keeping up with assignments. I loved my Bible classes and kept up by waiting till the last minute and pulling all-nighters to get things done.

In the meantime, our romantic lives were entangled in the turmoil of college life. Russ and I were dating on and off. I would be devastated because he broke up with me. Each time I was sure it was for real and that it was final. I would cry and scream and write poems and songs and manipulate him into coming back. Looking back, I'm really not sure why we had all the sturm und drang. Our backgrounds were very different. I felt I needed a lot of attention and it became overwhelming to Russ. We also had a lot of good times. I tried a hundred times to say, "Jesus is all I need. If Jesus isn't my first love, then nothing else matters." But I still worked to get Russ back. Pete was always my best friend and was there to hear my woes. I suspect he probably heard Russ' too, but he never broke confidences.

When Russ and I were traveling, we tried to be careful to avoid even "the appearance of evil," as the Bible says. Certainly we expected that people knew we were not sleeping together. Occasionally this became awkward for churches that booked us for a weekend that was away from Azusa Pacific College and from our dorms. Many times these churches were having a guitar played at their church for the first time and they were horrified that two boys, 18 and 19, and two girls, 15 and 18, were traveling together without a chaperone. We truly thought very little of it. We slept in sleeping bags on people's living room floors or crashed in seats of our cars if we got sleepy on the way home. No big deal. As far as life at Azusa was concerned, there was a curfew for the girls' dorm, but not for the boys. I found that appalling. The worst violations of the curfew that year did not come from us, however. I heard about a honest-to-goodness panty raid that some of the boys made on the girl's dorm rooms. Oh, scandal!

I was a complete conundrum to Prof. One time he told us we were doing a concert with a reception afterward for some people who supported the concert choir. He told us the girls had to wear dresses (below the knee, but not granny dresses) or a pants suit. If we elected the pantsuit, the top had to come below our derriere because "a woman never knows how she looks when she's leaving."

I headed off to Sears. None of the women's tops fit me. I went to the men's department and found a lovely purple t-shirt. It was a heavy material so it would not cling to me. Prof. didn't like things too tight, and it was long enough to cover my derriere. Perfect, I thought. Then miraculously, I found a pair of purple tie-dyed pants the same shade of purple as the t-shirt. I matched perfectly.

I had a 40-inch waist and 34-inch inseam so the pants were a real find. I think I did wear shoes, but they may have been flip-flops or tennis shoes. I put my long hair up in a ponytail and used two extra-long bobby pins to pin it under, since Prof required women's hair in an up-do. I donned the outfit and headed for the concert and reception, certain that I looked entirely appropriate following all Prof's rules.

Prof. was clearly horrified and positive that I had done this as a rebellious teenage miscreant trying to outwit and torment my elders. Prof's scowl was legendary. He directed us by it many times. In fact, I was fascinated by the fact that choir would be singing beautiful, classical praises to our God and the audiences could see our smiling faces and only Prof's back. But while we were smiling, Prof might hear an error or see a face failing to smile. He would point an angry finger at us and make the most dreadful, hateful, glowering frowns at us, which the audience never saw. I always wondered what might have changed had there been a camera on Prof's face. I couldn't tell whether his deep affinity or all things proper would have caused him to change his scowls, or whether the audiences would have had a different perspective of our performances.

On the Day of the Purple Pantsuit, Mrs. Anderson, who was universally called Mrs. Prof, pulled me aside. She explained the meaning of "pantsuit" to me and told me there was another whole department at Sears for fat women. Since the fat men's clothes were in the same department as the other men's clothing, this had never occurred to me. She explained it was on a derent floor entirely and that I should shop there for some appropriate clothing for choir events until we had our own gowns made. It turned out I wore a size 24, which I'd never heard of, but I found the department and complied with the request.

Prof continued to harbor deep doubts about all of us in Children of the Day. He was uncomfortable with Wendy traveling with us because she was so young. He was uncomfortable with Russ and I being so publicly physical, certain that this meant "free love" still reigned in our private lives, as well as the lives of Pete and his girlfriend, Wendy Lynn. He was disapproving of my background with drugs and each time I stayed up all night to complete a paper, he thought that my red eyes or sleepiness portended drug use. No matter how I tried, I seemed unable to please Prof. Ironically, the one place I truly shined that semester, Concert Choir, was the only "C" reflected on my undergrad grades.

Because we had been so steeped in 'the Word' at Calvary Chapel, most of the Bible classes seemed very easy. Studying the teachings of the "Great Church Fathers" was odder to me. It taught us how doctrines of the Church had changed over the years, conforming to the customs of various cultures. It made it easier to see that historical situations that seemed horrendous in retrospect were not made in huge leaps, but in tiny steps.

Studying the Church just before the Reformation I was aghast at the idea of purchasing forgiveness from corrupt priests who robbed the poor and frightened, and catered to the rich and arrogant. I also understood that this started out as a very small thing; people believing that penance should "hurt" somehow; and that just saying, "Oh I'm sorry about that," was inadequate for some sins. This also meant that Jesus' atonement was not enough. It meant that salvation could not really be a free gift and that we must somehow earn it. Scripture seemed clear enough on that subject, but a very small and very human impulse started the Church on a different path. I could picture that a very slight, one-degree different path led to a vastly different end and wondered what in my life could do that.

Once again, it was a first for me to find that Christians disagreed on what I thought were basic doctrines. Finding that there were teachers who disagreed with us on doctrines that we found central to our beliefs was baffling, and understanding how they could consider themselves "real" Christians was eye opening. One of our professors did not believe that the baptism of the Holy Spirit was anything separate from salvation. Having a prayer language and other "miracle-working" was not for today, according to him.

The many concerts that Children of the Day did for Azusa Pacific exposed me to some very different ministry than we had seen at Calvary Chapel. I think one of the distinctive customs of Calvary Chapel is that most of the pastors and teachers speak in the same voice and manner on "stage" or in the pulpit as they do off of it. This subtly inferred, to me at least, that their lives, and ours, should be the same in church and out. I think it was a huge draw to hippies who were constantly looking for what was "real." That meant that many of the typical conservative "evangelists" of that day were completely dismissed by us.

One such evangelist at the time was Marjoe Gortner. He was a well-known Southern Gospel-type evangelist. He had been preaching since he was a young boy with much hype about the fact that he started so young. He came to Calvary Chapel and spoke to many of the kids. He told us he was making a movie and he wanted to include us in the film. He said it would be a big draw to our church. Although being in a movie sounded cool, the idea that we needed a "draw" was sort of ridiculous. We had outgrown our new sanctuary in just a few months. We stretched out the sidewalls of the building and filled those seats too, then put chairs outside on the lawn and went to three morning services on Sundays, so that part about being a "draw" wasn't seductive to our thinking.

Marjoe began bringing around little "contract releases" for us to sign. Many of the kids weren't old enough to enter into a contract. Papa Chuck put his foot down, though. For one thing, he was very protective of this fledgling little flock. But the other point he noted was that those "little contract releases" all clarified that none of us, including Pastor Chuck, could have any final say in the content of the movie. Chuck was adamant and Mr. Gortner moved on to another Santa Ana church. As it turned out, the movie was just called "Marjoe" and it showed him "preaching." He screamed and shouted and jumped around and quoted Scripture right and left. He waved his arms, and the people in the congregations were depicted as just as excited and wound up as Rose Bowl football fans. They screamed and shouted and "fell out" as he yelled out warnings about hell and condemnation. Then he took up the collections. He talked about how much they were willing to sacrifice for the Lord. He quoted "freely ye have received, freely give," and told them they should give.

But even as they were collecting money, he filmed himself "backstage" or out of the pulpit area in a back room, mocking the people who were giving. He talked about how all this preaching was just so much hype to get money out of gullible saps and made bets with his backstage crew about how much more he could collect from an already downtrodden crowd. It really was a sad and intentionally shocking movie by a man who called himself an atheist in the film and showed himself a shyster with easy-to-fleece sheep. It was also one of the many times that built our trust in Papa Chuck.

No one hyped anybody up or screamed at us in our services. We didn't even take "collections." Money was not a big subject. We all learned that "to obey is better than sacrifice," and that the Word taught that if everyone simply gave 10 percent of whatever income they had, then there would be enough for the church to minister in the community. There was a box in the back of the sanctuary where we put our tithes and offerings and few of us struggled with that. We were always sort of excited to see what God would do with what we gave.

There were a few times that Children of the Day had a "tithe" that we felt led by God to share with someone else. I remember a very pregnant waitress who served several of us after a church service. We shared about why we were there and what Jesus meant to us. Then we prayed about it and left our tithe for her. She sat down at our table and cried. We joyously informed everyone about it the next time we were at church and it was freely affirmed that we should always do as the Holy Spirit directed us to do with money.

Papa Chuck and his wife, Kay, lived in the same tract home and drove the same cars, at that time, when they had 250 people in church as they did later when they had 10,000. So the example that we saw was very low-key on "fundraising methods."

We continued to struggle through the crazy schedule at Azusa Pacific, and Calvary Chapel continued to grow. We met with the other music groups at Calvary to talk about our new albums and discuss how to sell them. There was a GLASS convention coming up (Greater Los Angeles Area Sunday School) and they wanted us to bring our records there to sell. We tried to talk about what seemed right to us. One of the guys pointed out that people would be using credit cards to purchase our music and we weren't sure if that was good for Christians to go into debt to be able to listen to our songs. We really had never thought about "appealing to our audience." We just wrote what was in our hearts and this whole idea of our ministries being a "business" was foreign to our thinking. At the time, we ended up not bringing our albums to the convention because we felt that "suggested donations" were a better standard for making our music available.

We also spent whatever free time we had helping out at the church. Calvary Chapel was building again, providing outdoor space for the overflow of kids at church. We all pitched in doing whatever we could. As the concrete was being poured for the extended patio, one of the local drug dealers and some of his friends came by, essentially to make fun of us. We weren't all that bothered by it, but Chuck, ever shielding, walked by us with a wheelbarrow full of stuff. He kept the stunning smile on his face as he walked up to the mocking kids. "Any of you want to pitch in; we'd be happy for the help. We've got a lot to do." He took hold of the wheelbarrow and with his arms extended lifted the whole thing up in the air to his shoulder height and leveled a stare at the gang. They suddenly found something very interesting to do elsewhere as he set it back down. In retrospect it was sort of a goofy thing to do, but I loved it that someone wanted to protect us.

# 11
# OUR FIRST INTERNATIONAL TOUR

As the choir's summer tour approached, we began to try to figure out how we could all go. The offer had been made to have the choir do a set, and then Children of the Day would do a mini-concert, depending on the time allowed, and then have the choir do the final set. Wendy was going to be allowed to come. The choir was booked for concerts in several US states, in Canada and seven European countries and for the First Jerusalem Conference on Biblical Prophecy in Israel.

The only hitch was each student had to raise funds for themselves. We had some help from our parents, but not nearly enough. Papa Chuck was completely at ease when we told him, though. He felt sure it was the right thing for us to do and quietly explained our opportunity at a church service. They took up a love offering for us. It was enough to cover the trip for the four of us and we started to pack.

At the time, I think Russ was the only one of us who had ever even been out of California. The rest of us had a couple of quick tourist trips just over the Mexican border to Tijuana but that was it. Most of the world seemed like a fairy tale or a movie set to me. On the other hand, the four of us had certainly been more exposed to the ways of the world than some of our very sheltered classmates who had rarely been away from their parents' direct supervision. Prof Anderson and his wife, "Mrs. Prof," had minimal help from some of the other older students in choir as chaperones but a great deal of our time was on our own and we interacted with people and customs of other cultures as fairly brash young Americans.

The part of our trip across the US and even into Canada did not seem all that different from home. The sites were beautiful and our hosts gracious but it felt like many other trips we'd taken to various churches. The first real comeuppance we ran into was in England. We had been invited to sing at one of the chapels at Eton – a school that had educated several of the Archbishops of Canterbury, English poets and politicians and some of the original signatories of the US Constitution. The students there were very much like we were – occasionally rowdy and good-natured about a bunch of foreigners on campus. Although most wore suits and ties everywhere, the suits were fairly rumpled, the ties untied, and we liked getting to know them. But when we told them this was our first trip to Europe several of them asked, "Really? When are you going there?" This was long before the European Union, of course, and we didn't realize folks in Great Britain did not consider themselves part of Europe proper.

We continued to run into customs similar to our own but different enough to be offensive. One of the guys in our choir gave a huge yawn one morning before we had adapted to our time changes and people turned away in absolute disgust that he had not covered his mouth or stifled his yawn. One evening at a restaurant a waiter actually took the bread roll out of my hand, set it on my bread plate and tore off a small bit of it to place back in my hand. This was to demonstrate my manners in that regard were found wanting. I contemplated explaining it was bad manners to tell someone they had bad manners but felt both overcome by my own paradox and embarrassed that anyone had to speak to "the fat girl" about proper ways to eat.

A huge surprise at one hostel where we stayed was "the California Platter" which several of us eagerly ordered. It turned out to be buttered white toast tips around a plate filled with pureed spinach with a lightly boiled egg floating in it. Nothing I've seen in California before or since.

More serious faux pas were to follow. Several students had parents who had always been their moral guides and decision makers. They found lots of novelties that could have been dangerous.

It was legal to sample the German beer, to go to "health spas" where men and women bathed together and wore no bathing suits and to find the streets in Holland where living women displayed in the windows were for rent by the hour. It was illegal, of course, to buy hashish in the taxi station in Haifa, but some of them did that too. For the four of us, whatever wild oats we might have had we had sown long ago. They actually held very little interest for us other than our concern for our friends.

Here we were singing in magnificent cathedrals many centuries old, where Bach or Brahms or Beethoven had played. We enjoyed seeing not just cuckoo clocks but also the little Swiss chalets on which they are modeled, watching Waterford crystal glass be cut, or eating the most famous chocolate in the world. But we still sometimes behaved very much like arrogant American teenagers with a sort of entitlement to be in each setting and with little sensitivity for the cultural norms different from ours.

At every concert, we ended Children of the Day's set by singing *"For Those Tears I Died."* I continued to be astonished, partly because it persisted in deeply touching people's hearts, but also because, even in Europe, some people already knew it. I now began to hear the chorus in different languages. It always touched me.

One turning point for me was our trip into East Berlin. Most of my life, I had read about the Berlin Wall and the people who escaped over it or died trying. Only recently there had been a story in *Reader's Digest* about a man who had built a hot air balloon surreptitiously in order to escape with his family one night. He ended up willing to jump out himself as ballast to allow the rest of his family to escape. When we learned we were to be allowed to tour East Berlin behind the Wall we were astounded. It turned out the plan was for us to leave our own tour bus and belongings and board an East Berlin tour bus with a special tour guide and driver. We would then tour the city, have lunch there, and return to our bus in West Berlin on the other side of the Wall.

Prof. had many rules to discuss with us about our behavior on this part of the tour. We would not be singing and he told us it was "not protocol" to be "witnessing" to the East Germans. He also told us what questions we could and could not ask of our tour guide. One of the more boisterous choir members, Rick, said, "Gosh Prof. I'd hate to be in heaven and see this line of people who never met Jesus getting ready to go who-knows-where and have one of them say, 'You're that college kid I met in East Berlin. How could you have known about Jesus and not told me?' I can't imagine just telling him it wasn't protocol." Prof. grew red-faced and sputtered but did not really give him an answer.

Once we got to the border, we carefully boarded their bus. Oddly, they searched underneath the bus with mirrors mounted on long handles – as though people might be trying to sneak IN to East Berlin. That mystified us but shortly we were distracted as we passed by the "tank barriers." They looked almost like picnic tables turned upside down in deep trenches but they were intended to stop tanks from plowing down the Wall. We passed through the gate into East Berlin and we could see soldiers on the roofs of the buildings with machine guns smoothly keeping us in their sights until we passed all the way into the city.

As we came into the city of East Berlin, several of the houses looked especially grand with turrets and balconies and beautiful front yards. Rick, our troublemaker, looked over his shoulder and quickly pointed out the view to several of us. These "houses" were facades, with only a single wall facing the street, propped up by several long pieces of wood.

To those of us from southern California they looked exactly like a television or movie set intended only to be seen from the front. I know the tour guide was talking as we drove but the things we saw were more powerful. I remember little of what we were supposed to be looking at. We saw tiny little kids – maybe 5 to 7 years old – marching in formation. We saw a huge billboard with only a raised fist pictured on it. There was German writing on it none of us could translate.

Our guide was conspicuously silent on the great television tower East Germany had erected directly next to what used to be the highest point in all of Berlin, the cross tower at St. Mary's church. Proudly looming over the church was what the West Germans called Fernsehturm's Folly. It seems the great multifaceted dome of the TV tower showed a huge cross whenever the sun hit it. So no matter where we went in East Berlin a bright cross shone over us. The television tower was supposed to show the superiority of "man" and technology over the "ancient mythology" of Christendom. The story was the East Berliners had tried painting it, tilting it slightly and replacing the mirrored facets with flat surfaces but, whatever they did, the sunlight caused the bright cross to shine.

Finally, the guide asked if there were questions. Prof's burning glare kept most of us quiet but Rick could not contain himself. "So, if this is such a great place to live, why is there a wall to keep people from leaving?" Silence fell immediately on the crowded bus. "Well that's a simple question to answer," the guide said easily. "The Wall is not to keep our people in. You see, we have a very solid economy and financial system in our country and the Deutschmark here is far more valuable than the one in West Germany. The only reason for the Wall is to keep our economy stable by keeping West Germans from coming in and spending their money here where they could get far more per Deutschmark than they can in their own country."

Rick followed up quickly, "Then why can't your own people leave?" The guide shot back, "Well of course they can leave. It's no different than how you in America have to go through a process to get a passport and travel papers before you travel abroad. There's simply a system our people go through to get passes to travel."

The conversation stopped there. We could hardly argue we had read in *Reader's Digest* no one could actually obtain those East German passes. But we all knew. The tour continued and, the further we got into the city, the more oppressed we felt.

When we finally stopped for lunch there were other East Germans already in the diner. Russ and I ended up sharing a table with a man dining alone. We were able to piece together enough conversation with our sketchy German and his fairly good English to understand he had a wife and three children. He eventually understood we were in a Christian choir from the US doing a concert tour. He asked if we were singing here and we said we were not. Then he said, "So you are just leaving when your tour is done?"

I was instantly struck with the understanding this sweet man, a human being whose hand I could reach out and touch across the table, would have given his life to have his own children hop on a tour bus and leave East Berlin. My casual entitlement of being an American, with freedom of movement and of choice, suddenly showed itself as an enormous ingratitude in my life. I thought of the popular protests of the '60's and how I had claimed myself to be "down on American imperialism" without ever having any idea what imperialism actually was. The whole place began to feel crushing to us and we got back on the bus anxious to leave. When we hit Checkpoint Charlie and saw the Marines standing guard to be sure we got safely into free territory, I cried and vowed never to be ungrateful again.

All throughout the tour, we saw hearts touched and lives challenged and changed as we sang. It was at once the expected result and a shocking miracle each time. It seemed, no matter where we sang, people responded and I was beginning to hear stories about how *"For Those Tears I Died"* had touched people I had never met. One man shared with me he first heard the song behind what we then called "the Iron Curtain" in an underground church in Czechoslovakia, another was in a church in Hungary where they felt they sang the song at risk to their own lives. I couldn't imagine being a part of something so huge in God's plan.

If we had been given tough instructions in East Germany, there were even more as we flew into Tel Aviv. The 1971 Jerusalem Conference on Biblical Prophecy was at the end of our tour in Israel. There we would hobnob with Prime Minister David Ben-Gurion and 1,500 delegates from 32 nations. Carl Henry, the editor of Christianity Today, had arranged the conference and the Israeli government provided the hall free of charge.

We sang with the choir and did our shorter set as Children of the Day but we heard other fascinating speakers. Hal Lindsey had just published his book, *The Late Great Planet Earth*, one year earlier in 1970, and it had sparked much discussion in evangelical circles.

Pete and I talked about how glad we were Israelis seemed to know we were "for" them, we understood their fears, we supported their safety, we believed in their God. We heard speaker after speaker talk about the prophecies concerning Israel becoming a nation again, the repossession of territory recently regained, and the prediction a "power from the north," which everyone seemed certain meant the United States, would come forward.

We heard Israeli scholars, both Jewish and Christian, confirm the generation that "saw these things" would not pass away before Messiah returned. The only question seemed to be whether a "generation" spoken of some places in the Bible meant 40 years or whether it was a generation like those of the unbelieving Israelites wandering in the desert so many thousands of years ago. In that situation, every person (except Joshua and Caleb) of that "generation" had to die before the promise of a new land could be fulfilled. We were absolutely positive, right along with every speaker there; in 1971 the Lord's return was imminent. But for us, the conference was not the most memorable part of our trip.

Touring Israel

The entire choir started with a tourist's journey of Israel. While we expected historical sites and biblical stories we were unprepared for the emphasis on Catholicism. We visited the Church of the Ascension, the Church of the Nativity and the Church of the Annunciation. Since we were clear in our minds no one could specifically tell where these events actually occurred, especially the ascension and the annunciation, to us they were no different than any Catholic shrine anywhere in the world. Another choir member asked me what "the annunciation" was; I told him it was supposed to be the place the angel Gabriel told Mary she was going to be pregnant with Jesus. Prof. was irate. Apparently one was not supposed to use the word "pregnant." I never knew if that was because it was church, it was Catholic, or just because Prof had an old-fashioned opinion about it like his ban on long hair hanging loose on a woman.

Children of the Day ended up hustling through the pre-arranged tours so we could get back to the hotels, grab a guitar and take off. We sang in pubs, which were much more like a Starbuck's than like any bar. We talked and shared and laughed and met dozens of people who said they just wanted us to love Israel like they did. No one was offended we were Christians. We sang our songs. We sang folk songs. We sang the Israeli national anthem, *Hatikvah*. We got to see their homes, the sites important to them and beautiful views of the Sea of Galilee.

In fact, one morning when Wendy left the hotel very early to watch the sun rise over the Sea of Galilee, she got lost and forgot the name of the hotel we were in that night. A member of the Israeli military picked her up and patiently drove her up and down streets until she recognized the front of our hotel. She also wrote one of my favorite songs, *"Be Ye Still,"* on the shore that day.

One night we waited until everyone else was in bed and snuck out to the taxi station at the Haifa gate. Most of the people there were Arabs, some Christian, some Muslim, but we sang and laughed and shared until after midnight. Poor Prof. was sure we were up to something nefarious, but truly, we were in love with Jesus and wanted to talk to everyone about all He was doing in our lives. Every time an Israeli Jew would say, "We just want you to love Israel like we do" we felt just the same way about our own newly found Messiah.

On the final day of our formal tour, we were antsy. Seeing one Catholic shrine after another was not on our wish list and, at the last stop of the day, I was in a big hurry. This, at least, was not a shrine but a fairly recent archeological dig. While most of the Garden Tomb was excavated by the 1920's, the nearby Damascus gate had only been excavated in the early 1960's, just a few years before we visited. So the pathway leading up to the tomb was still rough and ancient looking, like so many things in the Middle East.

As I hiked hurriedly up the path I found myself alone and was struck with what it must have been like to be one of the women in Jesus' time, visiting the tomb: running along, in a rush and wondering – even doubting – whether all you knew and believed in was dead and gone. Were they dreading what they would find? Were they still hoping it wasn't true? What would it feel like to put all your faith in someone, to "bet your life" He was the One, the true God, only to find Him dead?

I found myself filled with dread, almost reliving their panic. The last few feet, others from Children of the Day caught up with me and we rushed into the tomb. We were supposed to wait outside with the others, to hear the story of the Garden Tomb and its bona fides for being the true burial place of Jesus. We noticed a few things. We did have to duck to get in – didn't Luke say the apostle Peter had to stoop to get in? But mostly we actually breathed a collective sigh of relief. I know it sounds silly but we were all so grateful it was empty.

Each of us had felt empathy with people from 2,000 years before who had run up the same path. In the end, it didn't really matter to us whether this was the "actual tomb" where Jesus' body had been laid. For whatever reason, God had chosen to bless this place. Wendy and I talked about it later and we both felt it was the place we had most palpably felt angels hovering around all the people gathered there. I wrote a song *"Easter Morning"* about it later with input from Russ and Pete, about how hard it was to realize, that on the first Easter morning, there was only a group of completely hopeless stragglers who had lost all they believed in.

We left all the more convinced the story we told was real. We knew God had made real changes in our lives and would create that same new life in anyone who looked to Jesus for healing and salvation.

We had a few days "on our own." We sang in more corner shops and taxi stations. I dressed up at an outside bazaar as a Bedouin woman in robes, complete with sash and dagger. I realized how hot this clothing was. Finally, we went to the "Wailing Wall." I don't know the answer now any more than I did then about what God's will is in Israel today. But you could hear the heart of people crying at the wall. There are only about 13 million Jews in the world and almost half of them live in Israel. They are still acutely aware of the fact a third of all the Jews on the earth were killed in the Holocaust. Rather than the large families they used to have, the culture has changed to having only the number of children you can personally protect, which usually means two.

We had seen the tremendous hospitality of the people, their pride in protecting us. Here we saw their grief. At the time, it was still possible for non-Muslim tourists to go into the Dome of the Rock, built in the 7th century. It is built on the site of the Temple in Jerusalem where the Holy of Holies existed.

The temple was destroyed in 70 A.D. We knew it was a place of prayer, of grieving and of incredible power for most of the world's religions – about 3 or 4 billion people. Judaism and Christianity hold the stone in the center is the rock where Abraham offered to sacrifice his son, Isaac. Islam teaches it is the stone on which Muhammad stood when he ascended into heaven.

The locals told us the site of the mosque was actually chosen by a Jewish rabbi who had converted to Islam. The Hasidim, and some conservative Jews, teach none of us should be walking around, even by the Western Wall, since no one knows where the Holy of Holies is and we might inadvertently walk over the holy place. I'm not sure how appropriately awed we could be still in our teens, but it was overwhelming, and we left more certain than ever that Jesus' physical return was imminent.

We "knew," as often only young people can, we had the inside scoop on what God was "really" doing on the earth. I also remembered when I stopped partying and taking drugs in high school, my friends would look incredulously at me and ask, "You don't smoke or drink or do drugs? What do you do for fun or excitement?"

Certainly, my life could not have been more full of fun and excitement. While some of the members of the choir considered this their first time of "freedom" away from their families, we felt God was flinging us around the world from country to country to share the Good

News while there was still time. I was blessed to share in this tour and experience these things that many will never experience. God had much more in store for us as we started for home.

# 12
# KATHRYN KUHLMAN SHOW

It was during our return across Europe (I believe we were in Norway) when someone from a television station in the US got in touch with Prof. Remember, this was long before cell phones, so someone had to go to a lot of trouble to find us. It seemed Kathryn Kuhlman was doing a television special series on the Jesus Movement and wanted Children of the Day there to sing for the filming.

Kathryn Kuhlman was one of the very few well-known female evangelists in the 60's and 70's. She had started preaching earlier than that but had become more visible with evangelistic meetings in Carnegie Hall in New York and in the Shrine Auditorium in LA where she was compared to Aimee Semple McPherson from the turn of the century.

Kuhlman had been interviewed in *Time* and *People* magazines and on *The Tonight Show with Johnny Carson;* she had met with the Pope. At the time she contacted us she had a weekly TV show on CBS. She flew the four of us home to California for the taping. You can see excerpts from that series of shows on YouTube if you search for Kathryn Kuhlman. http://www.youtube.com/watch?v=Np8GJGZ3Vv8

We flew home in what had become our typical flurry of activity. Ms. Kuhlman was gracious and clearly delighted and overwhelmed by the presence of so many "Jesus People." She had invited many of the youth from Calvary Chapel, including our beloved Lonnie Frisbee.

We had heard her speak on television and seen people make fun of the dramatic elocution with which she spoke. I know I actually expected her to use an entirely different speech pattern "off stage" than she did on camera. But when we were introduced to her she declared her pleasure in meeting us in very formal tones. When my sister and I asked where the ladies room was, she flung her arm fully extended in the direction of a hallway and said, "It is they-ah." We heard later, or perhaps I read it in her biography, she spoke that way to overcome a speech-impediment from childhood. In any case, we came to accept her way of talking as "real" for her.

During the taping, she asked us questions that sounded a bit like a set up to us, such as, "And who is the very most important person in all of your life?" to which we all dutifully answered, "Jesus."

*It reminded me of an old joke about a Sunday school teacher who asked her kids, "Now children, what can you think of that is gray and has a bushy tail?"*
*Silence.*
*"Oh come on, kids, gray, has a bushy tail and lives in a tree?"*
*Nothing.*
*"I know you can tell me the answer to this one. What is gray, has a bushy tail, lives in a tree and stores acorns in its cheek for food?"*
*Finally, one little boy raises his hand and says, "I know the answer is supposed to be Jesus...but it sure sounds like a squirrel to me!"*

In spite of her questions, Kathryn was clearly so taken with us we all loved her. Our hippie preacher friend Lonnie Frisbee fascinated her even though Papa Chuck and some other ministers were also there. Lonnie was probably the gentlest of all with Kathryn, dutifully answering her rhetorical questions until she finally looked at his hippie clothes, sandals and long brown hair and asked, "Lonnie, are you trying to look like Jesus?"

He smiled and said he knew a lot of people who looked pretty much like he did, but then gave his stock answer, "I guess there's no one else I'd rather look like, though." This delighted Kathryn and the audience.

Lonnie had a purity of heart that touched many people in a surprising number of places. And his ministry work always demonstrated the love and power of the Holy Spirit was present. Our songs on that show were a little extra special that day.

# 13
# JESUS PEOPLE

Let me step back for a moment and put all that was happening in the larger context of the times.

The "Jesus People" appellation was fairly new, actually. We had not known what to call ourselves. The Time magazine cover in June of 1971 gave us the label. The other articles in that same magazine talked about whether Nixon should visit China and if we would ever do trade with them, how we could end the war in Vietnam, admissions of hundreds of women in France who had undergone dangerous and illegal underground abortions, and the strong opinion that Governor Jimmy Carter had no chance at all of being the nominee of the Democratic party because he was clearly unelectable as President. Dissidents actually marched in full view of presidential venues and carried out "sit-ins" on college campuses. But Jesus made the cover and we made the news and got a name for our new life: Jesus People.

We were caught up in the excitement of this new life, and it was impossible not to feel the bigness of it when we stood on the beach with thousands of teenagers and young adults there to be baptized. Children of the Day would take our acoustic instruments to the beach on Corona Del Mar's Pirate's Cove. Russ sometimes played the stand-up bass right out on the sand, and we would play praise songs all day long while young people waded into the ocean with Pastor Chuck, Lonnie and other ministry leaders, to be baptized. It was powerful.

Those baptisms, along with the Conference we had just attended in Jerusalem and the teachings we heard each time we went to Calvary Chapel, combined to make us certain Jesus' return would be within the next few years. At the very least, we were determined to tell everyone we could about His soon return while we still had time. Back then I could not have imagined I would be writing about this over four decades later.

Believing the end was near gave us a burning sense of mission and urgency. As a group, we decided to drop out of Azusa Pacific and go into ministry full time. Wendy was able to transfer the credits from the college classes she had audited and the papers and research she did while on the choir tour, to Claremont High School. She graduated at age 16.

The leaders at Azusa did all they could to dissuade us from leaving. The music department head, while acknowledging Pete's considerable talent, told him he "couldn't know what he didn't know," without finishing a music degree.   The President of the college enumerated for us the reasons we should continue. Prof. Anderson seemed disgusted we would leave, stating we were "quitters." He said people had believed Jesus would return "soon" since the church began nearly 2,000 years ago. None of them addressed how we could continue the grueling schedule required for keeping our scholarships and still find any time to study. This did inform our decision. We were singing so many times a week while in school. What could we do if we went into ministry full time?

We continued to attend Calvary Chapel at least weekly when we were in town. By that time Calvary Chapel had started one of the first "lending libraries" of recorded messages so we kept up with their style of Bible Study by listening to messages on cassette tapes. Generally, Sunday night Bible studies went through the entire Bible about every two years. The Sunday morning message would be gleaned from that week's reading, and Sunday night would actually go through those chapters explaining and analyzing them and how they applied to our lives.

Throughout the week Monday and Thursday evening Bible studies at Calvary Chapel Costa Mesa would go more thoroughly through one book of the Bible at a time, so we might spend a few months going through the book of Romans or Acts. Pretty much all of the ten thousand or so people who were at church every week knew which 10 chapters we were studying on Sunday night. Although some historical or societal context was given, the emphasis was always on how these scriptures related to us and to our current lives. It was a wonderful, if childlike, way to learn the Bible.

# 14
# PAPA CHUCK'S VIEWS

While the teaching at Azusa was solid and expanded our understanding of the history of the church and the development of theology, I could not have asked for any better foundation in the Word of God than what I received at Calvary Chapel. Lonnie Frisbee had opened our minds, touched us, inspired us and answered our personal questions. But Chuck Smith had a different impact on us.

As our pastor, Papa Chuck had very firm beliefs but he never seemed put-off when we had our own understanding or applied something differently than he did. He did sort of have the "final word" on many things in our ministry but, it was really because we deferred to him, not because he demanded it.

Papa Chuck did not hold a college education in high regard, though. He understood and approved of our decision to leave school and do music ministries full time. He also knew about the turmoil in my relationship with Russ but never commented on it unless I asked for advice.

On the other hand, Papa Chuck was very irm in his understanding of men, as in "male," not as in "human," being in leadership. Women were not even ushers or deacons in the church since Paul's epistles indicated deacons should be the "husband of one wife" and generally have their houses in order. For a while, this also precluded anyone who had been divorced or remarried, as well.

Pastor Chuck told us clearly he felt Pete should be the "leader" of Children of the Day. Russ handled that with equanimity, especially since he'd been in the Pete Jacobs Quartet. I think he felt disappointed from time to time that Papa Chuck never seemed to quite fully appreciate the strengths he brought to the group. Russ made sure we carefully and legally cared for ministry funds. He got Children of the Day approved as a tax-exempt organization and filed all the papers with the state. He continued to meticulously handle all of the finances for the group and kept track of inventory and royalties.

I moved into an apartment in Orange County with friends. Four young women shared the apartment and we worked at various jobs. We usually brought home whatever we earned and put it all in a drawer in the kitchen. When rent was due, or groceries were needed, we took money out of there. As far as I know, none of us especially noted who put in or took out more or less than others. You can understand what a good thing it was when it came to our music ministry, our ever-practical Russ took care of finances!

My parents continued in their alcoholic illnesses. Occasionally my father would alternate between being proud of our accomplishments – even claiming some ownership of them - and dismissing us as too young to understand life. One time he came to a concert Children of the Day did at Calvary Chapel. Afterward he was walking around telling people, "Hi. I'm Ed, the father of Children of the Day." When he said it to Lonnie Frisbee, he received a different reaction. Lonnie turned without missing a beat. He took my father's proffered hand and said, "Nice to meet you, Ed. I'm Lonnie, the son of the King."

# 15
# TRAVELING

Our first on-the-road vehicle was a former bakery truck, similar to an ice cream truck. We packed our sound system in the back and all crammed in one way or another to travel to concert sites. I didn't find any of that too odd for the first couple of years, but later when Russ and I were married and I was pregnant and still sitting cross-legged in the back of the bakery truck, I was less patient with the arrangement.

Nevertheless, we saw amazing changes in people. It seemed each time any of us sat down to pray with someone to ask Jesus into their hearts, we all had some small worry about whether "it would work" this time. Of course, God always "works." We found, just as in Jesus' parable, the seed, meaning the good news of Jesus' life, teachings, death and resurrection, fell on some ground that was ready for it and it sprung up to life and produced its own fruit. Some seemed to grow up, but withered quickly with nothing to nourish or water them, and some simply fell on the hard soil of people who thought we were idiots. The good thing was we were very clear on the fact we could not tell who would and would not really hear and receive what we were saying, so we said it the same to everyone.

Sally was a friend of Pete's who waited to see how this new life affected the rest of us before she committed to it herself. Pete was anxious to introduce her to Jesus, but he recounted to the rest of us how scared he was when she bowed her head and said, "What should I say?" Pete watched with trepidation as she made her way through her first conversation with God, but when she looked up at him, he could see in her eyes that Jesus had already taken up residence.

Some experiences on the road were simply hilarious – things no one would have believed if they were written into a sitcom. For instance, the group had met a couple who did prison ministry. Whenever we went to the prisons with them, we had to meet up with them off of the prison property and follow them in so we were sure we were following all the rules and had the proper paperwork. They always apologized they could not pay us for our ministry there, but the wife was a self-described "Avon Lady," so she often brought us gifts and samples of hair products or skin care. We tried to let them know we were happy to be able to minister and were very grateful for her thoughtful gifts.

One time we had planned to meet the couple at a rest area off the highway just before the exit to a prison where they had arranged our concert. We got there a few minutes early and saw the car pull over in front of us. Pete hopped playfully out of the van and ran up to their passenger window. As the woman rolled her window down, Pete burst into a spontaneous song about "wanting our shampoo!" The words had just left his mouth when he saw it was an entirely different couple and they were staring mystified at him and the van full of hippies with him. The man driving started to ask Pete for directions somewhere, and then thought better of it and screeched off, just as the "real" couple drove up to meet us. The extreme humor of the situation did not quite strike Pete as immediately as it did the rest of us, but "I want my shampoo," became synonymous with being in a socially awkward situation.

We had been on the road for several months and we were singing at a crowded church service when Wendy and I were both struck by a family sitting in the 3rd or 4th pew. Afterwards we shared our thoughts with one another. It appeared to be a wife, husband and two children. The kids were very into the music. The woman laughed and listened at the appropriate times, but seemed a little sad. The man looked outright bored. He was just this side of rolling his eyes and shaking his head at most of the things we shared or sang. Pete gave an especially poignant altar call that night, giving people the chance to "say yes to Jesus," and many people came forward to pray, but the man we had noticed stayed resolutely in his seat.

For over a year Wendy and I prayed for that man; that "face in the crowd." I wrote a song about the experience and when we returned to the church a year later, I explained a little about the song's origin. I never identified who the person was, and I didn't know his name. But the man was there that night and came up to us in tears. He was so touched that we noticed him, prayed for him and remembered him when we returned. It seemed odd to us since he had appeared so callous on our first visit but, he became an ardent supporter – both of Children of the Day and of Jesus.

**Face in the Crowd,** *Marsha Stevens, copyright Capitol CMG*
*I caught your glance through a sea of people.*
*You understood the words I shared,*
*As I looked into your piercing eyes I saw no peace, and you were scared.*
*The thing I knew you'd never see was the whisper of my silent prayer.*

*(Chorus)-Oh won't you please, please say yes to Jesus,*
*You've played the games, you know you've lost,*
*And through all the pain and sorrow, when all the coins have been tossed,*
*You know the cost; it's been paid in full on the cross.*

*Your head was noddin', your feet were tappin',*
*The girl beside you seemed to know,*
*In the sundown of your dying story there's really no place left to go,*
*But even when you know you need Him that final step can be so slow.*

*(chorus)*

*And when at last we all were prayin' my closed eyes still could see your face,*
*I only hoped when it all was over that great change would have taken place.*
*The games you knew would always beat you,*
*Your fear-filled eyes could see His face.*
*(chorus)*

I was thrilled with every person who decided to become a follower of Jesus. We never saw anything inappropriate about the way numbers were quoted by evangelists, like "10,000 people came forward at the Billy Graham crusade", or by the book of Acts, "the number that heard and believed was about 5,000." But I was always struck with the individual stories we got to be a part of through our concerts.

# 16
# MARRIAGE

In 1971, Russ asked me to marry him after we finished the college tour. I accepted and I was so happy to be marrying him. He was gentle and composed and, since he had never seen his parents fight, I just knew we wouldn't either. Friends who knew my past would tell me they understood why I loved Russ so much, especially since he was nothing like my father. They felt I was "breaking the cycle of abuse" by marrying him.

We were the first of our friends to get married and neither of us had any idea how to plan a wedding. We were both 19 years old and I knew Russ' parents worried about us. They had married young themselves so they no doubt knew some of the perils and difficulties. They could see the vast differences in our backgrounds. His parents were educated but also very much self-made people. I always joked that between the two of them, they could have been stranded on a desert island and rebuilt civilization. Russ' Mom was the go-to person for anything you ever wanted to know about making and keeping a home, cooking, sewing, gardening, decorating, cleaning, pest control, or etiquette. She was ready and willing to help me.

His Dad had helped Russ build his own car, understood construction, electronics, sailing and navigation, plumbing, fishing and music. He also sang in wonderfully entertaining Barbershop Quartets. My daughter still sings Barbershop (Sweet Adeline's) in her grandfather's honor. Both of Russ' parents seemed to observe the world with a *joie de vivre*. I was so excited to be marrying into that kind of a family.

The wedding was to be held at Calvary Chapel, of course, with Papa Chuck doing our ceremony. I was fairly horrified to find out my father expected to participate in the service. He was still a licensed minister; but I didn't really want him to participate in our wedding.

However, Pastor Chuck invited him to do the opening prayer and that seemed to settle the matter.

As the time drew near I had a friend sewing a dress for me and I was determined to lose weight for the wedding. We tried to nail down details. I weighed well over 200 pounds when Russ proposed and was substantially below that for the wedding. Happily, it was on one of those reasonable eating less/exercising more regimens, so I felt healthy. My roommates pitched in, but my sister Wendy helped most. We found flat ballet shoes so that I wouldn't appear to be taller than Russ.

His brother and my sister were best man and maid-of-honor. Russ' father planned a rehearsal dinner for us. Russ and I worked out our wedding ceremony. I saw the ceremony as a sort of magical event. I mean, the two of us were about to become one. I expected to leave there an entirely different person.

I meant every word of every vow with all of my being and I was very aware I was "swearing to God" for the first time in my life. My father's opening prayer was full of, "We beseech Thee that Thou wouldst..." etc. But the rest of the ceremony was our own and from our hearts. I had big dreams for our life together. Papa Chuck always tells personal stories during weddings, and he did that with us. Russ sang in his high sweet tenor and I just knew we left different than we had been when we arrived.

We honeymooned along the Pacific Coast Highway, starting in Solvang, a small Danish town along highway 101. We were self-conscious newlyweds and a maid inadvertently walked in on us, much to our horror. But later we laughed; the honeymoon went better after that. We ended in San Francisco, one of our favorite places, and had a lovely time. When we got home we discovered Pete and Wendy had done most of the moving into our new apartment for us and so that made life easier as we began to set up house.

Five weeks after the wedding, I discovered I was expecting our first child. Russ was sweet, he cried, we were both thrilled. If he had any doubts about our readiness to raise kids, he never expressed them to me. His parents were cordial but surprised. I was completely clueless they might be worried about our youth. My parents had a completely different reaction.

Together they set out to change their lives for the good. Clearly, they felt, with a grandchild, they might have a chance for a clean slate. Both of them rededicated themselves to the Lord. The group was getting ready to go on tour again and, when we left, we were more hopeful than we had been in a long time about my parents' commitment to turn their hearts to Jesus.

Just as my parents were getting better, we found to our horror some of our other friends were simply deciding to return to their old lives. We did not feel judgmental, nor did it ever occur to us God was angry with them or going to punish them. We were simply heartbroken, devastated that drugs or alcohol or old wounds created a rift for them they were not able to bridge.

Besides the songs we were writing to express our love for one another and our courtships, we were writing songs of lament about our friends who had decided Jesus was a silly myth or an unreachable Judge. In response, Wendy, Pete and I wrote songs for them with love and longing.

# 17
# ON THE ROAD AGAIN

We had been singing every month or so for hymn-writer and evangelist Audrey Meier, who wrote *"His Name is Wonderful."* I remember singing for her gathering the first time. We closed with *"For Those Tears I Died,"* and she asked us to sing it again. We did and she turned to me with a line she was famous for, "Ohhh, I wish I'd written that!"

We met and sang with Andraé Crouch and his twin sister Sandra at one of Audrey Meier's services. Andraé made most of his appearances as "Andraé Crouch and the Disciples," however the Disciples turned out to be mostly Sandra and whatever other fabulous musicians and singers happened to be around on any given day. They were the first group we met who already traveled the way most mainstream artists do, in a real bus, and who had booking agents, publicity agents, publishers and so on. They were wonderfully kind to us though we were about 10 years younger and very green. In many ways they took us in to give us guidance in keeping a Jesus-centered life on the road.

A big part of this tour was to be "Explo 72". This was a 6-day event in Dallas sponsored by Campus Crusade for Christ. There were daily meetings, seminars and mini-concerts, and every evening we met in the Cotton Bowl. Part of Wikipedia's description of the event says, *"Billy Graham spoke on six different occasions during the event including the final event which was a public, eight-hour long, Christian music festival on Saturday, June 17, 1972. It was dubbed as 'The Christian Woodstock', and the event drew an estimated attendance between 100,000 to 200,000."* Newsweek described the crowds as being 'militant Christians.' The featured artists included: Love Song; Larry Norman; Randy Matthews; The Archers; Children of the Day; Johnny Cash; Andraé Crouch and the Disciples; and Kris Kristofferson. The festival was held on a huge open swath of *land just north of downtown Dallas. That area had been cleared for construction of the Woodall Rodgers Freeway.*

*"The excavation for this highway linking Interstate 35 and US75 would forever obliterate the festival site. Many conservative Christian groups were critical of Explo '72 for its ecumenical involvement with both Protestant and Roman Catholic ministries, and for its use of rock music." (Wikipedia)*

We sang one night just before Kris Kristofferson, however, we were much more excited about meeting Billy Graham. We also looked forward to hearing Larry Norman, Andraé Crouch, and friends from Calvary Chapel again. The Cotton Bowl was so packed we couldn't save our own seats or get out front to hear, so we watched from backstage and some nights from under the stage. One surprising thing I learned at Explo '72 was how much less nervous I was singing for a hundred thousand people than I was singing for 20 people in someone's living room. It was almost impersonal with the headlights, spotlights and footlights blocking our vision on stage and the people seeming so far away when we did get glimpses of them. But I was still honored and humbled to have that same hundred thousand young people singing the final chorus of *"For Those Tears I Died"* with us at the end. It felt like a little foretaste of seeing us all around the throne one day, singing praises together.

Mostly we had fun with the thousands of new young Christians gathered there. Somehow Children of the Day lost our backstage passes and Andraé Crouch was quick to get us back into the area for performers. Wendy says after we all got professionally made up, trussed, and sprayed for stage, Andraé found her and told her, "Sister I hate to tell you this, but you are 16 years old and you look like a harlot!" This sent us into such hysterics Andraé decided he and Wendy should go around telling everyone they were engaged. We were, after all, some pretty socially liberal kids from California in a mostly white, southern, conservative area of Dallas. Several people were noticeably distraught to see a black man in his early 30's engaged to a beautiful blonde teenager. No matter how he was treated though, Andraé was always the picture of grace and he helped us learn the difference between being faithful to the ministry and taking ourselves too seriously.

The tour lasted 6 weeks and I was definitely "showing" by the time we got home. My pregnancy changed two people I did not think could change...

# 18
# FAMILY CHANGES

My mother had not had a drink since we left and she was reading her Bible for the first time I could remember. My father was trying to be patient and more forgiving. He was changing, too. Although I never did see him address any of his sexual addictions, he did get alcohol out of the house, which he said was in deference to my mother. Everyone was blessed and encouraged real change was happening.

I have to say that, although I was certainly glad for the big changes, it was hard for me not to think about my parents' love of alcohol during my childhood, *"If being sober is a choice, why wasn't I a good enough reason for you to get sober?"*

Those thoughts gnawed at me sometimes during the emotional and physical changes of pregnancy. I had "morning sickness" all day most days, which resulted in my gaining about 3 or 4 pounds during my whole pregnancy. I was very wary of taking anything for the morning sickness. Actually I thought I was probably still overweight enough the baby would get whatever he or she needed. This was still at a time when everyone had their regular family doctors deliver babies. We didn't see an Ob/Gyn doctor unless something was suspected to be seriously wrong. So I was given prenatal vitamins and lots of encouragement but not a lot of other information. Generally, I loved being pregnant. As much as I still hate to admit it, I did love all the attention I received. Everyone was excited.

We continued to tour throughout my pregnancy and I bounced around cross-legged in the back of the tour van or bakery truck. Pete got engaged to a girl he knew during high school, Hanneke, and they were married toward the end of that year.

The song Pete wrote for her, *"If You'll Take My Hand,"* completed the three love songs on our next recording which was called, *With All Our Love.* The album was released in 1973. Some of the other songs, as I said, had lyrics pleading with friends who had somehow chosen not to continue life as believers in Jesus, *"Where Went the Days"* and *"Just Pretending."* And of course we recorded Wendy's beautiful song from the Sea of Galilee, *"Be Ye Still."* All of our songs were deeply rooted in personal experiences.

With so little familiarity with childbirth in our circle, we had booked another tour a few weeks after my due date. But I was two weeks late and while it was possible to do a few songs without me, it wasn't going to be possible for them to do that without both Russ and me. My family doctor told me that sometimes drinking castor oil would start contractions.

Two hours later I was in labor. Russ was great; carefully following every Lamaze rule we had learned and practiced including reminding me that we should just call these "contractions," not "labor pains." I was livid at the lovely lie this would not hurt if we called it the right thing. I didn't care what anyone called it, this was P.A.I.N.

The doctor, who had told me it would be hours yet before I delivered, hurried into the room, was shoved into a gown and gloves and sat down at the foot of the bed just in time to catch our baby girl. Naomi Joy was perfectly quiet. She stared with clear blue eyes at the bright light over my bed. She was so still that everyone panicked for a few minutes. They went to suction her but could see she was breathing. They cut her cord, moved her limbs, examined her, then shrugged and handed her to me. I felt like she was born with joy.

All of the lack of drama at her birth turned out to be a foretaste of Naomi's childhood. She rarely cried. I could probably count on my fingers the number of times she cried in her first year. It seemed she never did anything until she could do it correctly. This meant she was late with several growth milestones. She waited to speak until she could say the sounds clearly. Sometimes I heard her practicing words in her crib but she would not repeat them to me until she suddenly could say that word with good diction. She didn't walk until she was about 14 months old. She never did the 'toddle and fall' routine to get from one place to another. Nor did she hold onto the furniture. She didn't walk until she could do it on her own.

Once home, I healed quickly. My mother stayed with us for a few days to help. Everyone came to see Naomi and without any fussing she went to any arms ready for her. We took her to Calvary Chapel, where about 2,000 people were then meeting in a huge tent while we waited for a new larger sanctuary to be built. Pastor Chuck had the church pray for us and dedicate her to the Lord.

After the service I let someone hold her. When I went to retrieve her, that person had let someone else take her and I followed anxiously from person to person until I finally found her at the back tent flap of the church, happily perched in Pastor Chuck's arms, sending everyone off with a smile.

# 19
# TOURING WITH A NEW BABY

Touring with Naomi Joy was a breeze. I was always with her, so it was easy to feed her every four hours. It never occurred to me to waver from that. At about 3 weeks she started sleeping through the night and I bottled milk with which Russ fed her as well. At concert venues, we simply asked someone in the front couple of rows to hold her, never thinking that anyone might be concerned that she would fuss or cry. She never did.

As hectic as it sounds, our lives were really pretty regimented. On the road we called it "eat, ride, eat, ride, eat, sing, sleep, repeat." We loved what we did. Our friends tended to be in other singing groups that toured. We knew the other groups from Calvary Chapel, of course. Love Song was a band that seemed much cooler than we were, with more rock, less folk and jazz. Other groups like Country Faith, Mustard Seed Faith, Debby Kerner, Selah; Blessed Hope and The Way, all were on the first released Maranatha! Music album *The Everlastin' Living Jesus Music Concert.*

We also renewed friendships on the road. I have great memories of just hanging out with Second Chapter of Acts as we continued to minister with them. One was watching how they rehearsed. As I said, Matt's voice was changing; many reviewers called his voice the most unique in all of Contemporary Christian Music. While I'm not sure there is such a thing as being "the most unique," his voice is amazingly expressive and agile. His work on it reminded me of the parable of the talents recorded in Matthew 25: 14-30 and in Luke 19: 12-28. The Scriptures told how the faithful servants multiplied all the Master had given them.

Many venues were continuing to do as had been done at Explo '72, booking many groups for one "festival" or "concert series." Maranatha! Music often sent several groups to one venue. And, by the time our second album was released, Hanneke and Pete were expecting their first child.

We found a way to keep singing but closer to home. We worked with theme parks in Southern California, like Disneyland and Knott's Berry Farm, to have all-Christian music nights. They were skeptical. No one had done that before and they were concerned with catering to what they still considered a very narrow audience at the time. We showed them we meant business. We sold out Disneyland on what was billed as the "Nite of Joy."

Many of us who grew up in the area loved being "backstage," which is actually underground at Disneyland. As kids we had all saved and traded shoeboxes full of ride tickets for Disneyland. They had A, B, C, D, and of course the famous E tickets, which were graded by the excitement and popularity of the ride. "A" tickets were for things such as the Cable Car ride down Main Street. "E" tickets were for the Matterhorn Bobsleds and the Submarine Voyage. Other rides were somewhere in-between those. But on these special venue nights, Disneyland had already started charging a higher price for entrance and made all the rides "free" or accessible for the one fee.

At that very first Nite of Joy, Children of the Day was part of the planning. We knew of Disney's conflicted feelings about hosting the night with all Jesus People groups. They reached out to one or two more classically "Southern Gospel" groups to try to broaden the range of people they thought might come that night. But the park was packed and truly joyous. Between singing sets, we would run out to get on a ride or meet friends for a bite to eat and then rush back to sing.

At the end of that first evening, most of the Jesus people bands stayed to pick up trash. It was SO important to us Disneyland feel they had made the right decision. Disney management told us later it was the cleanest the park had ever been left and they have continued to host Christian music events to this day.

# 20
# HAWAII

While staying close to home was a practical thing to do with a new baby, our group somehow had booked concerts in Hawaii. It grew out of a long desire to minister there. It was not a desire to get an all-expense paid trip to the beaches. After all, we already lived at the beach in Southern California. We later understood lots of people had wanted to be paid to go to Hawaii but just called it ministry! The local churches on the islands, with many low-income or impoverished families, were hesitant to provide booking fees or travel expenses to groups who wanted to "minister" in Hawaii.

We pieced together a tour, partly financed by supporters at home, and then we set off. We had space for a speaker/evangelist and we invited another young hippie from Calvary Chapel. Greg Laurie was kind and fun to be around and an entertaining cartoonist. He had put together some "tracts" we used in place of the sometimes extreme and judgmental Christian pamphlets put out by Chick Tracts at the time.

Greg's main cartoon character was "Ben Born Again," a cheerful, long-blonde-haired guy who looked a lot like Greg. While they were never deeply serious about one another, Greg's presence on the trip was wonderful for Wendy. They hung out together on the tour by default since the rest of us were paired up. Greg found Wendy charming and they had similar senses of humor. We were grateful for his healing touch with her. He was a great addition to our time in Hawaii.

We were especially thankful for Greg's evangelical spirit. We found there were several things we did that were considered ungracious to the "aloha spirit." For one thing, we took it as a matter of respect that we made every effort to start a concert right on time. This was just short of appalling to most Hawaiians who felt common courtesy was to give people time to gather and chat before settling in for an event. Things always started on Aloha Time. Greg would easily lighten our interactions making people laugh and loosen up.

Other churches felt it reflected badly on them when we sounded like we were sharing something altogether new and different since they felt they'd been preaching about Jesus for years. A few were actually not happy to see young people coming up to pray at the end of the concert/sharing time, dedicating their lives to Jesus. They felt it made the programs they had been using all along look meaningless if members of their church would feel the need to come forward and pray.

One girl who was 15 years old fearfully approached me and tried to stay out of the sight of others. She told me she was the pastor's daughter and, after many failed attempts to communicate with me, finally blurted out he was abusing her physically and sexually. She told me her mother knew but nothing had been done to stop her father. I was so young and so struck by her confession I was just dumbfounded. I had no idea what to tell her except God could see her through the next two years until she could get out of there. I held her, prayed with her, cried with her, told her I had survived the same thing, and hoped deeply it was enough.

One weekend on the island of Oahu, a church very casually cancelled our concert. We scrambled to look for housing and managed to find a hotel on Waikiki that would let us all stay in the room. Greg Laurie promptly dropped a power cord off the balcony and helped Russ and Pete set up the sound equipment out on the beach.

This was no doubt illegal but honestly never occurred to us. We started singing and drew quite a crowd. Then Greg got up to preach. You might think everyone vacationing on the beach in Waikiki would wander away at that but, it was a Sunday morning, and Greg was a riveting speaker. He still is. People came out on the balconies of their hotel rooms and as more people gathered, Greg decided it was time for an altar call. I want to say hundreds of people came up to pray with us, but it was so long ago. Let's say for sure dozens and dozens of people came up to pray. It seemed like an endless line. I'm sure Greg even baptized some of them in the Pacific Ocean that day. It was just like our baptisms back home.

It was dusk when we finally tore down the equipment; all of us feeling it had been a "God thing." It was beautiful to be there, spiritually and physically.

# 21
# HOME AGAIN

After we returned to the mainland, Greg traveled with us briefly but, before long, he got together with his wife-to-be and started teaching a Bible study at Calvary Chapel. Chuck had a rule that the people who wanted to get up in front of everyone to preach had to spend a certain amount of time cleaning the church and picking up the cigarette butts around the perimeter. He wanted to see they had a servant's heart. Greg certainly had one and shortly after he married Cathe he started a church in Riverside, California, called Harvest Fellowship. It was about an hour from the original Calvary Chapel in Costa Mesa.

Meanwhile, Calvary Chapel kept growing. The Calvary Chapel Board of Elders purchased property a block away from the little Chapel. It had been used for planting, mostly strawberry fields and was an enormous lot of land. It was on this new location where we pitched the huge tent.

Offerings and tithes, as I said, were discussed in a very low-key way at Calvary Chapel. We learned during our Bible studies "tithe" was defined as 10% but it was explained in the sense this was just how things worked - if everyone gives 10% of their income to charity, then everyone has enough. Since our Bible studies took us through the entire Bible, the scriptures about giving and finances seemed to come up naturally. When those of us in the church anticipated purchasing the new property, Pastor Chuck told the congregation he and the elders had prayed about the payments to the bank. They were wondering about the wisdom of being in debt and paying interest with our offerings. He asked us all to pray for wisdom.

A week later Shell Oil company approached the church about renting the space right at the corner for a large gas station. It took up only a small percentage of the lot and the payment they offered covered the church's payments to the bank. This was just one of the many answers to prayer we experienced and we were convinced that God could do anything.

When we erected "the tent", it was huge. We were proud it was put up by our own hands. It was, however, subject to the Santa Ana winds every few months. Nonetheless we had services every day and concerts every weekend there and thousands more young people surrendered their lives to Christ in this tent. Later the current building was erected along with Sunday school classes to accommodate hundreds of kids each week. Ultimately a Christian school was finished as well; kindergarten through high school. Children of the Day participated in all of this, ministering in music in each place. Calvary Chapel was our home and we were happy to devote time and energy as it became a well-recognized presence in Costa Mesa and all of southern California.

# 22
# SECOND EUROPEAN TOUR

We continued to travel and sing in a variety of places. In 1974 we booked another tour in Europe. This was our first time back since the choir tour. We visited several of our friends from other groups, some of whom were living in England at the time. They were gracious hosts and we sang for large and small events. We were still quite unaccustomed to other cultures.

One of my friends living in England was married to a musician but she was also a very accomplished seamstress. On her birthday, we decided to all pitch in and buy her a sewing machine. This would have been a very simple quest in the U.S. but proved to be an unusual item for the U.K. Apparently, professional tailors made most "homemade" clothing, and having a sewing machine in one's home was uncommon.

Russ and I searched all day, taking buses, taxis and finally a horse and buggy to an outlying village where we found a small Singer Sewing Machines store. Even then we were almost shut out because of our late arrival. The owner only relented after we showed him a fistful of pounds and promised to buy a machine. It was worth it. I can still see my friend's huge, tear-filled eyes as we brought it into the front- room. She had been understandably upset we were late for her birthday dinner. It would have been terrible to arrive late and empty-handed.

In Holland we stayed in Den Haag, or The Hague. Hanneke, Pete's wife was from the Netherlands and, of course, spoke Dutch fluently and did a beautiful translation of the chorus of *"For Those Tears I Died (Come to the Water)"* in Dutch. But there, we ran into other customs that blindsided us.

The family we stayed with fixed us traditional Dutch meals. At breakfast this meant "something on bread." The bread was either homemade or fresh from a local bakery with thick butter and a topping on it. The grocery stores had whole aisles devoted to things to put on your bread for breakfast, much like an American store might have an aisle of breakfast cereals. Dinner was sometimes rijsttafel or "rice table" which meant "something on rice." There would be a huge bowl of rice in the middle and they might serve a dozen small bowls of things like chopped nuts, pickled egg slices, coconut, curries, and peppers – anything to go on the rice.

One evening we offered to fix them a "typical American meal" and they were fascinated. We spent the afternoon shopping with the idea of a Denny's steak meal or a Sizzler platter with steak, potato and fresh salad. We were naïve about what they might actually enjoy! We had to go to a butcher to get the steaks and we had no idea what a "sirloin" steak was called there but we took our best shot. It was hard to find fresh iceberg lettuce, but we finally found a head and substituted other "salad bar" type items we thought would work well.

We prepared the meal and brought out the first plate to serve the man of the family. We had an 8 or 10-ounce steak for him with a large baked potato and a tossed salad in the middle of the table. We were proud of our efforts. The family - not so much.

First they were shocked to see all the expensive fresh vegetables in the bowl. When we set his plate in front of him, he laughed out loud and set it in the middle of the table. It took us a moment to realize this was the same to him as if we had set a whole Thanksgiving turkey in front of him. He took it for granted no one would eat that much meat alone. I think they were a little horrified when we brought out all the plates each with its own steak and potato on it. It was a great lesson for us in cultural differences. If we were seen as gauche Americans, they were certainly gracious to us.

The concerts continued to be well received. We had our first two albums with us that we sold at each concert. We also had royalties from other artists recording our songs or from radio stations playing them so we were able to support ourselves more consistently. We felt blessed financially. With joy we prayed with many young people at each concert. They were just learning the term "Jesus Movement" that had been used for some time in the U.S. They embraced the term and the way we presented Jesus in our concerts.

Back home, we had put in an answering machine before we left so we could have a record of calls that came in for concerts while we were gone. This was back when most people said they were "not going to be talking to some machine." It was a big deal at the time, both to have an answering machine and to figure out how to use one on the road. We also had to have some ingenuity about how to get people to use it.

We took one of the songs Pete and I had written, *"We're the Children of the Day,"* and altered it for our answering machine. The original song lyrics to the chorus were:

*We're the children of the light and we're the children of the day,*
*We need not always stumble in an ever darker way,*
*Though the darkness may close in around with shadows everywhere*
*Still Jesus Christ is in our hearts the light of the world is there.*

This was followed by a clever classical Bach-esque quartet that followed the same chord structure, but showed off both Pete's brilliant arrangements and the ranges of our voices. So we changed the words to:

*We're the Children of the Day and we are not at home right now,*
*But leave your name and number and we'll get in touch somehow.*
*Don't forget the area code and please speak clearly in the phone.*
*We'll call you when we hear it, just start when you hear the tone.*

Then we launched into our little "Bach" quartet. We got lots of calls and hang-ups from people who wanted to hear it. The problem was very few people left messages. We decided we had to hire a secretary to take the calls for us.

Our bookings increased right away.

# 23
# OUR FIRST HOUSE

By 1975, Russ and I were ready to purchase a house that had been donated to Calvary Chapel. Papa Chuck had been concerned when we first moved into it a year earlier that we might not be able to make timely payments with our touring schedule and ministry incomes. But even while we were on the road we had faithfully made the monthly payments and thought the purchase would be a simple matter. We had made improvements to the home, including finishing a room over the garage for the secretary who did our bookings. Russ and his father had worked on other projects, all of which had improved the value of the property.

It was the only time I really ran into the business end of that church. The men were considered the heads of the house and the family and women were to be submissive in all areas, including financial arrangements. Only the men in our group were paid. Wendy was still single and was paid separately but Pete and Russ were paid twice as much as Wendy was; Pete to cover his wife Hanneke and Russ to cover me.

Russ was a meticulous accountant and prepared papers for the Board of Elders at Calvary Chapel to enable us to purchase the home. These were the same men who had laid hands on Pete and Russ before we left on the last tour to ordain them for ministry. Russ and I had proven we could make the payments in a timely manner and Russ felt certain we could buy the house without difficulty and the money would be a blessing to the church. He even felt if we needed to get the house financed on our own we might do that as long as someone on the board cosigned the loan.

The meeting did not go as anticipated, and Russ came home crestfallen. He said the price of the house had almost doubled. When he explained we had tried to purchase it at the asking price a year before, the only caveat had been we showed we could make payments dependably, the men were dismissive of him. Now the board wanted a large down payment and twice the original asking price. When someone on the board suggested a compromise price. Russ was shocked when Chuck objected saying, "If you're going to sell it for that price, I'll pay cash for it for my own kids."

It was a rift that was never quite bridged. In time we would see what it did for Russ, who always felt overlooked by Calvary Chapel leadership. It broke any emotional ties he had there and allowed him in later years to move on into other ministry opportunities. But at the time, we were devastated. I was always glad I hadn't been there to hear the discussion myself since I still had Papa Chuck on such a pedestal. Russ and I found a less expensive home in Costa Mesa and purchased it with the help of a bank loan. We moved shortly afterward allowing Calvary Chapel to use the old property as they saw fit.

# 24
# WINNEBAGO

We continued to tour with Children of the Day. We had traveled in the U.S. and Canada in vans or cars. This was long before the days of cell phones and, getting separated was a problem, as was letting the other vehicles know we needed to stop. Wendy and I had a strong sisters' attachment and we usually traveled separately since we seemed to "just know" if the other one was in any difficulty. Looking back, it seems an odd approach – even a little spooky. But at the time, it was just a fact of life. We knew each other, and Children of the Day, as well as any traveling companions we had, counted on Wendy and me to know if the other vehicle needed help.

Ultimately, the group purchased our first RV. It was a Winnebago and its best feature was how many people could sleep in it. It was set up more like a tour bus, with multilevel bunks on each side of it. This suited us perfectly. The main idea was to have a way to travel together, cook for ourselves, and have a place for each of us to sleep.

Wendy had fallen in love with Kit Fremin, the groundskeeper at Calvary Chapel. He was far more than a handyman, with a love for gardening, and landscaping that kept the property beautiful. In exchange, he had been living in a small apartment in the church building. Soon, they were engaged to be married.

The group also surprised Russ and me with a gift for our second wedding anniversary. Pete said we had a concert in Los Angeles and we might have to stay overnight so we should all pack some light clothing. This was a bit mystifying since we drove up there in the motorhome but Russ and I complied. We were totally surprised when Pete drove to the Los Angeles airport and dropped us at the airport gate. The others in the group had purchased tickets to San Francisco for us to have a second honeymoon. We were very touched.

It was a great trip. We went to our favorite Japanese restaurant and wandered Fisherman's Wharf. Since we had not packed our birth control, we found out a few weeks later I was pregnant once again. There was a week's wait for the tests and as soon as I was sure I was pregnant, I started praying for a little brown haired, brown-eyed boy who looked just like his Dad. I really wasn't positive it was exactly ethical to pray for someone who was already growing in me, so I was careful to add in, "But Your will be done." We were still young and impulsive, but we really did want to be in the center of God's will. Probably Russ was more mature than I was and just prayed for a healthy child!

Our little band family was growing in other ways also. Wendy married Kit, who became our sound technician. Pete and Hanneke had a daughter. We continued to travel with many other artists. Karen Lafferty, who wrote *"Seek Ye First"* and other praise and worship songs, was one of our frequent companions. We continued to run into Andraé and Sandra Crouch, the Second Chapter of Acts and Love Song, as they were often ministering in the same places we were. Nancy Honeytree stayed with Russ and me for a while.

We ran into Larry Norman and met his new wife, Pam. They told about meeting one another and knowing right away this was "the right one." I thought they were probably just way more spiritual than I was. At least that's how I thought at the time. Jamie Owens was starting to sing separately from her parents, Jimmy and Carol Owens. Wendy and I wondered what it would be like to have a whole family who was following Jesus and singing together. A kind of 'Jesus People' version of the Von Trapp family (from *The Sound of Music*).

We traveled along as Debbie Kerner, whose voice I always envied, toured alone, and then with Ernie Retino as "Friends" and then as Debbie and Ernie Retino, "More Than Friends." Our extended family was precious to us and we encouraged one another through the struggles of life on the road.

At a concert at the civic auditorium in Southern California we were backstage tuning our guitars when the concert organizer told us "a soprano" would be opening for us. We must have looked quizzically at him since he began to explain to us what a soprano was. We knew perfectly well, of course, but it was such an odd way to describe someone at a Jesus Music concert. "A soloist" perhaps or "another act" is opening for you, but "a soprano?" When it turned out to be Sandi Patty, we understood the odd wording. She is much more than "a soprano," of course. She had not yet released her first recording, so she was playing the piano and singing on her own. She was magnificent. Over the years I've heard dozens of people describe someone at their church as "singing like Sandi Patty." Not too long ago I went with some family to a Sandi Patty concert where we sat in the front row so I could affirm to them NOBODY "sings like Sandi Patty."

When we were told "a pianist who someone had heard at Greg Laurie's church" would be playing at another concert it turned out to be Keith Green who had joined the Jesus People family. Keith was a challenge for other music ministers at times. He was incredibly talented, passionate and focused. His music and passion lifted all of us. He also had a very clear sense of right and wrong and he didn't see any reason why all Christians would not have a clear agreement with him on what was right or wrong.

Annie Herring from Second Chapter of Acts seemed to understand Keith's thinking but, for me, there were times that were painful and confusing. Some of it was social ethics. For instance, he railed at several of us before one concert because we were selling our albums. He said his were free because of the Scripture "Freely you have received, freely give." (Matthew 10:8) We countered that argument by saying "the worker is worthy of his wages" (Luke 10:7).

When he announced the free albums in the concert, people came up to his record table afterward and took away albums by the armful. Shortly they were gone. I didn't understand how that could be right for those of us supporting ourselves through our music. Even the apostle Paul seemed torn on that. He worked his own way through his ministry journeys yet, in his letters, told the churches they should be paying the people who came through working at their churches; that they were "worthy of their hire," and we tried to be worthy.

Plus, I always felt a little puzzled about how we read in the book of Acts the church in Jerusalem lived by all donating everything they possessed to the apostles who distributed it to each person what they needed. Yet Paul asked for offerings to be sent to the believers in Jerusalem in almost every letter he wrote, so I sort of wonder how that communal thing worked out for them.

Keith also felt we were not prayerful enough, had a spirit of levity, and were too focused on the business part of the music. In some ways, these were good things since it did keep us out of the mindset of "who has the best recording or the most airplay or the top billing." He reminded me a lot of John the Baptist – and if you think it would have been easy to hang out with John the Baptist then you should read about him again. I knew Keith was passionate and filled with a desire to please God, as were most of us, but it was also the first time I really saw people in music ministry so divided. Several years later, Keith wrote a letter to many of us apologizing for his judgmental attitudes and sharing how God had enlightened him in that area. I actually got it in the mail at the most shattering time possible - the day Keith was killed in an airplane accident with two of his children. Fortunately for all of us, his passionate music lives on.

# 25

# HEALING FOR MOTHER

**M**y father died soon after Naomi was born. Both of my parents had seemed to turn their lives around and then both of them became ill shortly afterward. My mother had a spot on her neck and a tumor on her lymph node that turned out to be melanoma – a particularly virulent cancer.

My father had a stroke. We were notified of both while we were traveling in northern California. Russ' best friend, Bruce, had us flown home in a private plane.

What Wendy and I found strange was as we asked one person after another to pray for our parents, the prayers seemed to take a certain form. Over and over again the person praying would pray for healing for our mother and God's will for our father.

This was before there were even prayer chains on the phone, let alone on-line, so it was not that people were conscious of praying the same thing. However, it was uncanny to hear over and over again, "God, we just ask your healing hand on Marsha and Wendy's mother, that You would touch and remove that cancer from her." Then they would continue, "And we hold their father before You that Your will would be done in his life, too." We found it puzzling, but we were grateful for the prayers.

And that's actually exactly what happened. My mother calmly went back to her doctor. He was ready to do exploratory surgery, remove all the cancer and do full-thickness skin grafts on the areas affected by melanoma. She told him she thought she'd been healed. The doctor tried to humor her but explained she needed the surgery anyway. You don't just wait and see with melanoma. She asked him to do another biopsy. There was no cancer.

He had the original biopsy retrieved from the lab, thinking there had been a lab error, but the margins of that sample were malignant and were verified to be the samples from her. He told her he had never seen a miracle in person and required her to return every two weeks, then every 6, then every three months, then twice a year. When she did pass away 25 years later she was still cancer free.

My father, on the other hand, had a severe stroke. Wendy and I had never seen someone after having a stroke, so his paralysis and inability to speak were frightening. He was in a wonderful hospital in Loma Linda and had great care, but nothing was making him any better. He regained his speech for a few minutes when he said goodbye to Wendy. Then he had a heart attack. It was 1974 and my father was 68 when he died later the night of his heart attack.

# 26
# DEALING WITH DEPRESSION

I had so many reactions to my father's death. I didn't wish him ill but I was glad I didn't have to deal with him any longer. What was startling to me was I had spent most of my life being angry with him - righteously angry. I somehow thought when he died, I would not be angry any more. I'm not sure how to explain it except to say I had long been mad at him and the "at" was very resolute. Now there was no "at." I didn't want to be an angry woman but I couldn't seem to find the off switch.

I had always been a person of deep feelings, even melancholy. In fact, there was a Christian personality test that was all the rage at the time which grouped people by their test answers and the answers of their friends into four groups; sanguine, phlegmatic, choleric and melancholy.

The group, and most people who knew us, decided the four of us in Children of the Day represented each of those four groups. "Sanguine" people are supposed to be impulsive, outgoing and charismatic. Although they need some alone time, too, they pursue many hobbies, leaving them if they become boring. They struggle with being on time and usually feel they know what is right. I can still see some of my sister in that. "Choleric" people are described in the book as ambitious and leader-like, assertive and prone to mood swings. This was how people saw Pete.

Phlegmatic individuals are fundamentally relaxed and content with themselves. They are receptive, accepting and may be shy, but often prefer stability to uncertainty or change. They are consistent, rational and calm and make good administrators. This would be Russ.

Then there was "melancholic" and I so hated being called that. I struggled so much with depression as a young person I couldn't stand the thought of melancholy being an actual part of my being. Everyone assured me this wasn't what it really meant but I chafed so much at the concept I wouldn't even read the description at the time.

It says, as I read it now, the melancholic temperament is fundamentally introverted and thoughtful. They are often perceived as overly pondering and getting rather worried when they cannot be on time for events (OK, I admit to that part). They can be highly creative in poetry and art and can become preoccupied with the tragedy or cruelty in the world. Often they are independent and perfectionists. One negative part of being a melancholic is they can get so involved in what they are doing they forget to think of others.

But as much as that description irritated me, it was probably because it was so true, and I did sink back into a deep depression after my father died. I simply had no idea what to do with all that anger. When I had found I was pregnant with our son, it probably saved my life. The songs I wrote for the third Children of the Day album reflected my struggles.

At that time, we were very well versed in the "lay down your life, take up your cross and follow me" thinking. I thought "dying to myself" was sort of somehow becoming someone else and we equated it to mean "becoming Jesus." I have to say this describes a theology I no longer embrace in the same way. I believe today God makes me someone new, but not someone else.

One song, *"Tried in the Fire"* expressed how I was feeling: *"Oh, kindest Father, I question You… I hate myself in my heart …So somehow God let me lose my life, In Your perfect will crucified."* But I couldn't see that hating myself was a reflection of depression, not my commitment to Jesus.

A duet I did with Russ, *"Where Else Would I Go"* has been one of my favorite Children of the Day recordings. It is based on Peter's words in John 6:67-68 when Jesus asked His disciples if they would leave

Him as others had and instead of saying, "Oh no, we love you!" Peter asked, "Where else would we go?" I felt like I understood Peter; no matter what I had to go through to follow Jesus, there was no turning back.

*Oh, sometimes I forget how much*
*You changed me with a single touch.*
*And when I start remembering, I see Your eyes.*
*And then I see the differences in my two lives...*
*I lived within a different world,*
*Had different thoughts, used different words.*
*I drank when I was thirsty then – different water.*
*I cried when I was lonely then – different Father....*
*Oh, Lord, where else would I go,*
*If I sought to leave Your path behind?*
*If I look around, see the hate abound,*
*No one else would take the time to find me.*
*No there's nowhere else to go.*
*(Complete lyrics online)*

Russ had no idea what to do with me and my growing depression. I think he was as supportive as he knew how to be, but I bewildered him. I did not go to my father's funeral because I was sick. To this day I don't know myself how much of that was psychosomatic and how much was morning sickness.

The anger directed at my father now seemed to hang over me like a sodden umbrella. I found my greatest terror was I would become just like my father. Most of my young life, people had told me I was like him. I think they meant poetic, dramatic, that sort of thing. My mother had said it to me in despair. She didn't realize, I'm sure, what a devastating thing it was for her to be angry enough to say, "You're just like your father."

When I was about 15, I had finally told her how I felt. It was in a very unkind teenager fashion and she never said it again. However, it was written on my heart and in my soul. He was angry, unpredictable, selfish, abusive, impatient and manipulative. I was "just like him" and I couldn't bear the thought.

While I was pregnant with Johnny, our sweet Naomi, who was almost two, was beginning to exert her own will. The first time I actually felt angry with her, I came undone. It wasn't that I showed her my anger but, feeling it, I thought, "Really, how could I put my children through that kind of childhood? *I am* just like my father!" I withdrew so far into myself Russ took me to a psychiatrist who attended Calvary Chapel. I was fairly unfamiliar with psychiatry. Even then, the psychiatrist was the physician who ordered meds and someone else did the counseling.

It was 1974, and I was hesitant to go to him simply because I was embarrassed. Good Christians were supposed to rejoice in all things, not be depressed. Not only that, but I wanted very badly to fit in with the "older" women at Calvary Chapel. I was 22 or 23, so keep in mind the 35 year olds were the big, popular kids to me!

I wanted to dress like them and be thought of as a peer. I saw the psychiatrist's wife as the kind of person whom I wanted to approve of me – she was in the "in crowd" at Calvary. She and the doctor had just purchased a home on Linda Isle, a very exclusive area of Orange County. I remember being astounded their payments on the house were $2,000/month. I can't imagine what they'd be today. She served on the Women's Board, which was the only place where women were allowed to serve. She also knew everyone in the church. I was mortified to think she would see me as mentally ill. However, things had gotten too bad to ignore them any longer. I was cutting myself again, burning myself, rubbing soap in my eyes, just doing anything to get the pain inside of me to the outside. I needed help.

After a couple of attempts to do some kind of weekly counseling with a colleague, the psychiatrist suggested I voluntarily commit myself to Brea Neuropsychiatric Hospital. I was there just over two weeks, thinking surely there was some way to fix me. I kept thinking of television shows where the person has an "aha" moment and is all better. However, it became apparent to me this was not going to happen. I had no "aha" moment; I just sank deeper into depression. In some ways that was a good thing. I stopped waiting for someone or something else to make me all better but it also meant trying to take a real look at myself in ways I wasn't accustomed to.

The two weeks passed and we resumed touring and singing. Children of the Day sang at the Calvary Chapel Christmas Eve concert at the end of 1974 as we always had if we were in town for the holiday. My very pregnant belly kept bumping my guitar into the microphone, which had everyone laughing and right at midnight we sang *"Oh Holy Night"*.

At the time I still had a pretty strong high "A". Whatever the high note was, Pete arranged it so we changed to the right key in time to hit it which was very theatrical for us. Papa Chuck always said it was that high A that sent me into labor. I went home and woke Russ up two hours later to tell him "it was time." Russ said, "Oh you're just nervous because it's Christmas day. It's probably a false labor. Try to get some sleep." Two hours later I woke him up again and called my mother. She said the very same thing, "Oh you're just nervous because it's Christmas day. It's probably a false labor."

Two hours later I woke them all up again and called the doctor. I heard the same words for a third time; "Oh you're just nervous because it's Christmas day. It's probably a false labor. Try to get some sleep." They were all wrong. Johnny was born on Christmas morning, 1974. Naomi was sure I had brought home "Baby Jesus."

My son came out kicking and screaming and scarlet-faced with tight, tiny clenched fists. He was a stunning child. Photographers wanted to use his picture. But unlike Naomi, he did not sleep through the night at three weeks, or three months. He was colicky and wanted to nurse all the time. He'd cry so hard he'd throw up all the last feeding and want to start over. He definitely took my mind off of myself! The only thing that interrupted my trying to "get better" was having Johnny. I couldn't care for him and focus on my depression. He was very demanding of my attention. Russ and I were not prepared for the change in temperament. I don't think we ever really adjusted to how different Johnny was from Naomi.

Naomi was a happy big sister but her little brother showed his feelings very differently from the way she did. If she got sick, you'd find her curled up asleep on the sofa with her little forehead burning with fever. If he got sick, he'd awaken screaming in the night so we all knew he was miserable. Where she had waited carefully to do anything until she could do things well, he tried everything the minute he could. He walked early, talked early, ran early, read early, wrote early and rose early.

Johnny had some medical problems after choking on a carrot at a family meal. He needed extra care. We knew we couldn't leave our kids with just anyone who was kind and convenient anymore. One solution came from Toni, a friend from church. She agreed to rent a bedroom from us for a while as she needed a place to stay. Toni was a passionate new Christian who worked with mentally disabled people at a local hospital. She wasn't making enough money to live on her own yet. Russ agreed to let her rent his office space for a couple of months. She was a dichotomy of humility and entitlement. She felt it was obvious Russ should be willing to turn off a television show to give her ride to Bible Study. She would be upset if things didn't happen on her time schedule. On the other hand, it was a little more income for us and she had two friends, Marilyn and Karen, who felt God had called them to help with our childcare.

Marilyn and Karen were a huge blessing for our young family and they cared just as carefully for Naomi as they did for Johnny with his special needs.

One Sunday morning, shortly after Toni moved in, I got to church early so I could sit in the back corner where Kay Smith, Chuck's wife, and her friends usually sat. I waited eagerly for them to come in and finally the wife of one of the deacons came out and asked me to move. I told her it was no problem; I just wanted to sit with her and with Kay and that group. I scooted over in the pew. She finally told me, "No, this where we sit and I won't bring Kay out of the office and into the sanctuary until you move." I felt like I'd been kicked in the stomach and my face burned with embarrassment. I moved to a different pew.

# 27
# FOUND & LOST

I threw myself into helping Russ with the business details of Children of the Day as well as mothering Naomi and Johnny. Jesus Music was morphing into a full-fledged business by 1976. There were several record companies besides Maranatha! Music which started publishing what was just starting to be called "Contemporary Christian Music (CCM). Radio stations played it all across the country. Some Southern Gospel artists had started "crossing over" from old hymns to some CCM. Booking companies were formed just for the purpose of scheduling concerts for CCM artists. One of our friends, John Styll, started CCM Magazine in 1978 to promote the music and the groups.

As one part of my life was becoming more commercial, my older half-sister and half-brother came and went from my life one last time. My half-sister Kay moved into a live-in religious community that just called themselves "The Group." They became insular and Kay began to tell me I needed to move in with them. She said God had told her I would join them or "die in the wilderness" as so many of the Israelites had.

I lost touch with my half-sister and only found out after the fact she had died of cancer. While I lost her in one way, I lost Charles in another. He had worked in aerospace for several years before losing his security clearance over drug use. He became a professor at Cal State Fullerton and when I went there to visit him I found the students all loved Dr. Carter and seemed jealous I was actually related to him. My brilliant brother worked on many of the parts and calculations for the first Hubble mirror/telescope. But over and over again, the university paid for him to go through rehab. And, over and over, he lost his footing and returned to substance abuse.

It was heartbreaking for me to have him call me in the middle of the night too inarticulate to even complete a thought or a sentence. Eventually I had to tell him not to call me like that which I knew hurt him deeply. I just didn't know how else to disentangle myself.

The business aspects of our group travels were time consuming and also took its toll on my health. I felt like with the family separations and the struggles of keeping Children of the Day solvent, I was paying a price to stay on the road.

We continued to travel and sing, but I was presented with several health issues that put me in the hospital multiple times between 1974 and 1979. I had developed numerous ovarian cysts, starting before Johnny was born. I had subsequent adhesions (scar tissue) and ultimately required at least 7 surgeries. Today most of them would be simple outpatient procedures requiring a couple of Band-Aids, but at the time they were open surgeries and meant up to a week in the hospital each time.

I also continued to struggle with depression; I found I had to steel myself at times from actually hoping it was just time for me to "go home." I felt like I wanted to "be available" to death should it come around. The counselor/psychologist I had continued to see after the psychiatric hospital was convinced I needed to be proactive in fighting against those feelings.

Ivy was a therapist I had met at Brea Neuropsychiatric and she was determined to get me to conquer my depression. She would, for instance, insist I write down one good thing that happened during my every waking hour. Often, at first, it was, "The sun came up," which seemed like such a trivial exercise. But I really tried to shut a door in my mind on the negativity.

When I did, I realized there were many habits in my life that revolved around my depression. I didn't wear seatbelts or lock the door on my car. I walked next to the cliff edge on hikes and leaned out over a balcony to see one thing or another. It was risky and tied to that whole 'available to death' thing. I don't think I ever looked out of the window in a high building without at least a fleeting thought I could always jump. They were actually such subconscious habits I didn't notice them until I tried to stop them.

The counselor reacted very matter-of-factly about such revelations. "Hmmm, all very interesting but you need to stop that." It was a different approach to counseling I found more helpful for me than the standard, "let's rehash your childhood and all that's happened and see what the antecedents actually are for these feelings."

Ivy would emphasize, "Knowing why is the consolation prize." (Actually, she called it the "Boobie prize," but that may have been a slang term from my era, because people look askance at me if I say it that way now.) I'm sure that doesn't work for everyone but it did for me.

Along with the surgeries, I had what turned out to be a gallbladder-related problem. It's so awkward to write about personal episodes of health problems in technical terms. The reason this particular one is important was because it was a problem with a duct, attached to the gallbladder, rather than the gallbladder itself.

No one figured out the cause of my intermittent pain for several years. I'd go months or a year without it. It radiated to my back which also made it difficult to pin down. More than once I injured myself trying to alleviate the pain. Once I severely bruised my back trying to massage deeply enough to get to the origin of it. I think that behavior, along with my ongoing skirmishes with depression, led my family doctor to decide this was a psychosomatic illness and finally conclude it was a spiritual illness.

He came to me with his office assistant and said they had an important message for me. They had prayed about my illness and he felt the Holy Spirit had shown him this was a spiritual illness. There was something in my life for which I needed to repent. He was convinced this is what was causing my undiagnosable pain. I really wasn't clear whether he felt this was Satan causing me pain or God punishing me with pain. I always felt better about someone attributing an illness to Satan since the Bible is so very clear we have "victory" or power over the devil. So that was an easy fix, right? You pray and it's gone.

It was more complicated if he was saying this was God punishing me or "getting my attention" for unconfessed sin in my life. I have no trouble thinking of many times during a day when I'm "sinning" - I'm unloving, or not as understanding as I could have been, or less generous than I should have been or more impatient. I had no problem with repenting or turning away from those things and asking God's forgiveness. But the doctor's indication was this was a far bigger, more pervasive, more unusual, sin than that.

I stayed awake all night trying to sift through all the things it might have been. Sexual sins certainly came up for me but not as people speculated. I did not have a struggle with homosexuality; it wasn't even on my radar at that point. I thought instead of a scene from an "R" rated movie we'd seen. I wished I could erase it from my memory. Then there were the times when Russ felt I had been flirtatious or given too much attention to this guy or that.

As much as I tried at the time, I couldn't find anything outstanding enough to make me think, "Ohhh, that's what it is." Anything I could think of wasn't an ongoing sort of behavior, so stopping it wasn't an issue and asking for more forgiveness seemed counterproductive.

At that time, I also had several friends in a women's Bible study that really were resisting thoughts of sexual infidelity in their lives. One or two even talked specifically about looking at parts of men's bodies. They had shared about it in the Bible study and I was shocked. I really hadn't considered women had those feelings. I thought when women spoke about men's bodies (the very few times I heard any women doing that), they were sort of making fun of the way men ogle women and trying to turn the tables on them. It never occurred to me women were tempted or ogling the men.

What was even more surprising to me was several of the older, happily married women spoke freely of having moved through periods of similar feelings. They reassured the young women these were normal feelings and that, like the devil, they would "flee if you resisted them." James 4:7 (KJV).

Part of my horror wasn't just the thought women in the church were sexually tempted by other guys it was that the older women thought we might be having sexual thoughts like that. Most of the women had husbands in ministry. I wondered if anyone thought this had something to do with our relationships with our pastors. With Papa Chuck. Wendy and I both had very personal and tender times with him. There were times when we got to sit alone in his office to talk to him. Both Wendy and I had a reputation among our friends as excellent masseuses and would sometimes massage his shoulders while we talked. He was like a father to us, a mentor, a teacher. For me this was a wonderful gift, a time when I could give back even a little bit to someone who had done so much for me. It's something I still do for friends and has never been remotely associated with sexuality or sexually acting out for me. I felt sick anyone might possibly think about my relationships with Chuck or other ministers in that way.

I want to be clear Chuck never made me feel that way. He was always gracious and positive. In more recent years, some people have asked me about my relationships with men in my life and if I felt they were all generally tainted by my father. I don't think so. If they were tainted on my father's part, they were certainly as much healed by Papa Chuck's sure and certain loving boundaries. There was one instance when I could tell Papa Chuck was going through a struggle of his own. I knew he would never tell me about it and I didn't expect him to. I wrote a poem for him saying I could see the light in his eyes had been dimmed by something and I read the poem to him. We chatted, shared stories, I massaged his shoulders, we talked about Scriptures and quoted the poem "If" by Kipling together all the way through, laughing that we both knew it so well even though it ends with "And what is more, you'll be a man, my son."

As I left his office that day, he hugged me just a few seconds longer than he usually did and I remember just a wrenching heartbeat of fear, wondering if anything was wrong in our relationship. But there was not. He was the safe person he had always been and I knew I had not been misunderstood - at least by him.

# 28
# OUR LAST TOUR

We continued to have the opportunity to travel with many other artists. Sometimes, as in the case of Karen Lafferty, they traveled in the RV with us. Other times we traveled separately and we did a series of concerts together. I had the feeling we sometimes disillusioned people who traveled with us. We bickered like immature siblings. We didn't have group Bible studies on a regular basis and we failed to pray quickly enough when problems arose. I was very conscious I never felt like I was as "good a Christian" as others thought I should be.

Looking back, I have to say over the years I've heard about other groups experiencing drug abuse, alcohol abuse, sexual infidelities and financial misappropriations while in ministry. We were blessed to have missed so much of that. Our problems, for the most part, seemed very immediate. We got angry, behaved badly, apologized and forgave one another in fairly quick order.

In 1976 Light/Lexicon had approached Children of the Day about doing our future recordings and purchasing publishing rights to our current ones. It was a difficult decision in some ways since Maranatha! Music had always been our home. However, Maranatha! Music had some of the same issues Calvary Chapel did, without the tender spirit in leadership.

I suppose Pastor Chuck was just as single-minded and there were rules – spoken and unspoken – we understood we were to adhere to. But Maranatha! Music had grown quickly and we were all pretty young and headstrong so when rules were imposed that had not been understood by everyone, we objected. We were told, in no uncertain terms, by those in Maranatha! Music leadership that to disobey them was to disobey God. God had put them in charge and we should do what they said.

In contrast, Ralph Carmichael and others from Light/Lexicon were adept at contracts and clarity so we opted to go with them. This had some interesting ramifications for us, both positive and negative. On one hand, they were experienced and enthusiastic. We signed the contracts at a dinner at the legendary Brown Derby, which was a very extravagant restaurant in Hollywood (now gone). We began to plan our next recording with a budget thousands of dollars greater than anything we'd done in the past.

On the other hand, we pretty much crossed over into the high-end marketing of Contemporary Christian Music. Concert booking was taken over by the same group that booked Andraé Crouch, Pat Boone and shortly after that, Debby Boone. Ultimately we had a separate company that did our press releases as well.

In 1977 our "Christmas Album" was rereleased by Light Records, however the spark was diminishing. We had recorded the Christmas album ourselves at Buddy King's studio in Orange County where we had worked with lots of other artists in the Maranatha! Music years. Pete produced the music and graciously let me claim to produce the vocals but, really, his ear was always at the helm.

The Christmas album was one of my favorites and included one of the great pieces we had sung in high school choir together, *Holy Radiant Light,* by Alexander Gretchaninoff. It was the last record where we got to wing it in the studio, borrow weird instruments and, have friends drop by to join in here and there. When we first released the Christmas Album, we were pressing it ourselves, so we chose a dark blue glossy LP cover specially embossed with silver. Our choice was soon overridden when Light/Lexicon re-released it in more traditional and, no doubt, less expensive Christmas colors.

Also in 1977 we, released *Never Felt So Free,* and, in 1979, Butterfly. These were the two albums we recorded for Light/Lexicon. Recording was a whole new experience with them. Specifically, sections of the LA Philharmonic came to play on our album and every part was written out note by note. Rather than us bringing photos our friends had taken, a whole promotional shoot was scheduled. Some of that difference was subtle. We formerly would have said things like "We want to be sure to share the joy of the Holy Spirit," or "If you love Jesus, notify your face." This time, there was more overt "Look cool," "Look contemporary," "Let's get a shot that will make people pick up your record off the shelf." This was a totally different mind-set for us.

Similarly, in the recording studio, instruments were not played by our friends, but by professional studio musicians hired by Light Records. We did not go in and bicker over how we wanted this or that song to sound because Light hired an arranger to do all of that. The first recording with Light, "Never Felt So Free," sounded wonderful and cost perhaps 20 times what any of our previous recordings had but it felt so much less personal. I don't know that any of us could have put our finger on the differences. It also became our last album as the original Children of the Day.

This was the first time we were conscious we were hobnobbing with stars. We were in awe of the company we were keeping at the time. In 1977, Debby Boone was just about to record "You Light Up My Life." Andraé Crouch and his twin sister, Sandra, had been our friends for years, but now we were recording for the same company. The Wayne Coombs Agency did our booking and people discussed openly such things as who would get top billing at a concert venue. We crossed over into a different kind of life. It was becoming more evident we didn't seem to fit very well.

In the early years of traveling and singing we were very clear whoever was "supposed" to be at the concert would be there. If there were 12 people we sang with the same energy we would have for 12,000. There was, of course, a special camaraderie that formed when thousands of people were singing our original songs right along with us. That dynamic was encouraging and invigorating. In contrast, there was an intimacy when there were only a few people. Sometimes when a church or venue lamented that they felt apologetic about not having a bigger crowd or not reaching more people, we'd say, "Hey, somebody was singing the night Billy Graham got saved." What we meant was we might minister to only one person that night but they might be the one to minister to millions.

Additionally, there were tallies of how many people came to our concerts and our agents talked about our "draw" or the number of fans we would draw to a venue by doing a concert for a church or an event. There was nothing wrong with those things on their own and I am aware of the reality of having to deal with the hard, cold facts of paying bills and meeting quotas. It just didn't feel like "us." Pete had been the first one of us to say, "Let's take a break from the road."

We had a group meeting, and of course, we'd had many of them. This one was harder though. One side was Pete was concerned that his wife and growing family were getting too little attention from him and too little time to find their own places in the world. Another side was each of us loved the ministry and we had the new companies pushing for growth, exposure, popularity and new goals. And we had an important tour coming up and people to whom we had given our word we would appear.

Pete's wife, Hanneke, had been relegated to the position of "whatever someone else is not doing" too many times. She had a servant's heart and was great with the kids and the varying cooking/cleaning chores of the road. She sang sometimes in my absence and had written songs with Pete that we'd recorded. However, there really was no place for her to shine on her own.

Pete and Hanneke had managed to buy their own home in Irvine, California but we were rarely there for them to enjoy it. Sometimes when we traveled, Hanneke and I would take turns flying with the kids so the children had one long flight to sit through rather than days of driving in the RV.

Eventually, Pete asked us for time away to settle things with his family. Instead, we voted to go on without him. In retrospect, I wonder if part of the reason we were so unyielding to such a request was we each were struggling in our own ways. I found staying on the road could be a way to avoid personal growth and the struggles of everyday growing up. After all, we had a mission, so why sweat the small stuff?

Russ and I had married so young and started a family so quickly that some growing up was sorely needed. We had a hard time even knowing our own needs, let alone communicating them effectively to one another. Once again, we sought out a counselor. Ultimately the counselor we saw had us make a list of ten things we wanted from each other. I only remember the first one on each of our lists, but even those were telling. I had given Russ the impression I had more respect or deference for Pete than I had for him. His first request was about me changing that priority. I was completely surprised by his request. I had no idea Russ felt that way at all.

This is a reflection, I think, of how personally out of touch we'd become with one another. Our one-on-one relationship had gotten lost. We worked together every day but always in a group. My first request seemed equally puzzling to him; I wanted more time alone with him. I'm sure he felt he was with me all the time.

We struggled to understand each other but missed the bigger picture. It's like asking someone to say "I love you". You can make it specific, "I want you to tell me you love me at least four times a day." But what you really want is for the other person to want to say "I love you." You want them to experience love for you, and there's no way to legislate that. It was a no win situation. So even as Russ and I set about following the other's requests we failed to hear the deeper concerns each of us had.

As a group, we did go on to travel without Pete. Things seemed even more strange and strained for all of us. We wanted to feel Pete was replaceable but, of course, he wasn't. We did travel with some wonderful musicians, among them Jeff Crandall, who went on to play with the Altar Boys, and Jeff Millenson who went on to play with the Liberated Wailing Wall and work with Jews for Jesus. Other Maranatha! Music keyboard players filled in and they were great musicians, but, they weren't Pete.

We tried to move from our folk/jazz origins to more rock music and also added drummers for several tours. Each of these people came with their gifts and each was a great blessing for us and for the people who came to our concerts. As gentle and original as each of them were, I felt like we had lost who we started out to be in our attempts to be "marketable" or "modern". We weren't playing only for Jesus any longer. We were also playing for our producers.

"Crossing over" was a hot term at the time. For those of us in Contemporary Christian Music it implied crossing over into a secular market. Some people seemed to do it organically while staying true to themselves yet still reaching a "broader market." There was even a derision that came into play for those who stayed more strictly to playing overtly Christian songs in overtly Christian venues. People called it preaching to the choir or "fattening the sheep," and the supposition seemed to be real Christian ministry was "reaching the unsaved" or the "unchurched."

In my own heart, I loved ministering to Christians. I know that part of ministry can be selfish, like wanting to be liked or understood. But in my experience, the "churched" or the "sheep" needed plenty of feeding of their own. Pastor Chuck used to point out shepherds do not beget sheep. Only healthy sheep can do that which is why Jesus said, "Feed my sheep." (John 21:17)

Over the years I've come to really love that calling and to understand a little better why I longed to write songs that encouraged other believers. I felt almost ashamed to admit I felt that way at the time. Reaching unbelievers seemed so much more important to the CCM world.

# 29

# BACK TO SCHOOL

I tried to go back to school and take music classes at the local junior college again. Without Pete to write the music to my lyrics I was lost about how to put them to a melody. It seems to me unless I can "hear" the melody for a song in my head at the same time I'm writing the lyrics I can't impose the music on the lyrics afterward. If I try to it sounds forced to me and unnatural.

I thought a songwriting class would help me understand how to make that transition. The class was actually shocking to me. I had been away from secular schools and also the secular music market for a long time. I had been traveling with a group of Christians for many years. I was very taken aback by how openly people in the class talked about their drug use or their one-night-stands.

Both the men and women in the class seemed to write songs almost exclusively about whom they slept with or with whom they'd gotten high the night before. There were lots of, "Hey, I forgot to ask your name," or "I woke up and he/she was already gone" themes. Several songs stated overtly, "I like having anonymous sex in the dark." It made me sad, so the first song I wrote for the class was called, "Loving in the Light."

*"You speak of love that has no ties,*
*Of love that leaves you free.*
*You speak of love you fall into*
*That comes quite easily.*
*You speak of love with pretty words*
*You whisper in the night,*
*But isn't yours the kind of love*
*That fades with morning's light?*
*The kind of love He offers will not fly away,*
*'Cause lovin' in the shadows is a lie anyway,*

*You're walkin' into night to start a long, long search for day,*
*But the darkness makes you blind,*
*And lasting love you'll never find*
*Till Jesus' brightness chases night away..."(full lyrics on website)*

It really was an example of what I sometimes did best, to just write songs about an immediate situation that opened people's hearts. I was aching for the men and women in the class to have a true picture of the best they could hope for. I think the class was stunned when it was my turn to share the song. There was silence and then there was a whole class hour of heated discussion. I loved this, sitting around and sharing about the God I know. When someone brought their god of "You're Never Good Enough" or "I've Just About had it with You," I could honestly say that was not the God I knew.

It was a great conversation. The teacher gave me a good grade... and then he stayed to pray with me to dedicate his life to God and ask Jesus to live in him, to know that kind of love. I ended up writing more songs in the class with the teacher. I wrote the lyrics and he wrote the music which sort of obviated my "plan" to learn how to write the music myself! But I loved the experience and I wondered how many other ways we might be missing to reach out to the people around us. This was not for the purpose of "crossing over into the secular market" but just staying in touch with the world I lived in every day. We continued to travel and minister at venues large and small.

I've seen many times in my life how easy it is for any enthusiastic group of people to begin to believe they were the ones who were going to change the world. They believe "everyone" has heard of their movement or organization. The Symbionese Liberation Army, the ones who kidnapped newspaper heiress Patty Hearst, thought with their notoriety the entire world knew of them and they would start a revolution. The Black Panthers felt they were strong enough and numerous enough to permanently alter the socioeconomics of the United States. Even the Beatles believed they would change the way we all related in the world. From the outside, I could see how each of these groups could feel that way. They surrounded themselves with their own members or their own fans. Then they made the assumption that the whole world was experiencing and interpreting things the way the people who surrounded them were. What I couldn't perceive was how that applied to us in the Jesus Movement.

One notable difference, which I still see, is after we left a location or a group of people the Holy Spirit was still there working in lives, healing hearts, revealing truth, and bringing wisdom. Week after week, month after month, as we traveled in North America and abroad, we saw groups of hundreds or thousands of young people meeting together, being baptized, and praising God. They were learning to live and love each other and those in the world around them.

Our feeling of the Lord's imminent return went beyond "this is what prophets said", or "this is what we had been taught." We were experiencing this new life all around us. It was impossible not to feel we were seeing the world change and we were there right in the middle of the energy of this New Thing. We knew the verse, "See, I am doing a new thing! Now it springs up; do you not perceive it? I am making a way in the wilderness and streams in the wasteland." (Isaiah 43:19 KJV.) We knew we were a part of it. This is what empowered and motivated us.

Contemporary Christian Music was really just taking on its own personality. In fact, CCM Magazine, launched in 1978, was the first time we had a print venue for advertising. It was also the beginning of "charting": the best new song, artist, radio station and so on. Like most insiders, we knew who had connections with whom in order to get nominated. We struggled again to stay "in the world, but not of it." At the same time, we had signed the recording contracts and the company had invested money in us. They had paid people to promote us, and had a reasonable expectation they should recover their investments.

We had traveled for years in the RV and had done our own bookings. The tour routes made sense for us, as we drove to Southern California concerts followed by Northern California, followed by Oregon and Washington and so on. Now we began to find the concert bookings drove the itinerary rather than the other way around so long drives became more the norm. Many times we would split up and part of the group would drive in the RV with the sound equipment and I would fly with the kids. I remember doing one flight with three kids under 3 years old, something I would never recommend to anyone.

But all these things deeply affected both our camaraderie and the direction of our ministry. We began to be measured and evaluated by something other than the impact of our mission. Were we charting? What songs were getting airplay? Could we get friends to call in to the big radio stations and request our songs?

*Political influences*

At the same time, the politics of Christianity seemed to blossom. Where we once thought of politicians as fairly distant people for whom we were supposed to pray it suddenly seemed to matter what each one believed and how they voted. This was entirely new to us. I literally learned what "Watergate" was the night the president resigned. We did not follow politics. In some ways this made sense because most of us were not even of age to vote when we first came to Calvary Chapel. So the teaching there had very little to do with government representation. But this was beginning to change and people we knew had very strong feelings about the elections coming up.

Dr. Mark Allen Powell, in his book *The Encyclopedia of Contemporary Christian Music,* published in 2002, made this observation about that time; "Whether the Jesus Movement of the '70's morphed into the Religious Right of the '80's or was killed by it is a matter of historical perspective." All these things influenced our hearts and our ministry.

Other things were beginning to make an impact on the political scenery as well. "Gay Pride" or gay rights marches crossed our horizons once in awhile and Anita Bryant continued to be a personality who sometimes appeared near the places we did. Many years later, I met some of the people we had seen in those marches when Children of the Day was ministering in a park or outdoor venue. In fact, many of them became supporters and prayer partners in the ministry I would one day have to the LGBTQ community.

None of us thought very much about that at the time.

# 30
# MARRIAGE TROUBLES

Russ and I were focusing on our own relationship. We had tried hard to keep our relationship with each other. We had gone to a couple's retreat and worked on what it meant to say, "I love you," in our own languages – meaning, of course, we each show love in our own ways. When we still seemed distant, we went to a couple's counselor at Calvary Chapel. His style was very different for us. He said he would only speak to the head of the household which who was the husband in his view. The counselor felt this was Scriptural or at least scripturally oriented reading, I think, from Paul's epistle where he suggests women not speak in the church but go home and ask their own husbands any questions they might have.

When Papa Chuck taught about those passages in the Bible he put them in historical context. For instance, he pointed out women and men sat in different parts of the temple back then so, he reasoned, if a woman had a question she would have had to shout it out from where she sat and that would have created a chaos in the service. Nevertheless, at Calvary Chapel a woman could not be in any position of dictating messages or actions to a man. So women could participate on the Women's Board and be in charge of Women's ministry and children's ministry but not on the church board. There were no female deacons or female ushers.

This counselor took it all a step further and said he would counsel with Russ but I could be in the room. If I wanted to ask anything or say anything I could say it to Russ and Russ could either convey the answer to me or convey the query to the counselor. This turned out to be less than helpful.

We didn't realize we'd developed a "the show must go on" mentality about the ministry. This had the unfortunate effect of relegating our relationship to a back burner as well. I understand the theories

166

about how to develop priorities in one's Christian walk. Typically, the mantra is, "First God, then family, then work or business."

This was turning out to be an unhelpful model for us. What, specifically, does it mean to "put God first?" Does that mean start a day with prayer before anything else? Or reading the Bible more than you read any other book, or before you read any other book? Does it mean getting to the church service even if your kid needs you? Does it mean making it to the concert to share about Jesus even when you're withering away inside? Does is mean putting aside the needs of your spouse in order to preach the Gospel? I'm not being sarcastic. I really didn't know the answer. It's like saying "Well, just always do God's will," but how do you always know what God's will is? We both were trying to put God first. It was never easy to do that day in and day out.

When someone traveling with the group abused me I told Russ about it and asked him not to "over-react." I have no doubt Russ felt he was being understanding and forgiving with the person and doing exactly as I had asked. He did not address the situation or take any steps to protect me. I felt betrayed and hurt Russ did nothing about this person and continued to allow the person contact with my children and me. However, I really do believe Russ was trying to "put God first." There were other serious situations that arose in which we continued to misunderstand one another and distance ourselves from intimacy. We tried many "formulas" for getting closer or being "successful" in marriage.

Counselors gave us "exercises" which we dutifully performed but which didn't seem to make a difference in our relationship. I felt isolated and alone and counseling didn't change my feelings.

Russ had his own feelings of isolation to handle and didn't seem any better at it than I was.

This was especially true when we lost a friend. I knew that Russ lost friends in high school to sudden or accidental deaths. When we were married, the man he considered his best friend was Bruce

Bakalian. Bruce ran coffee houses called The Ark and The Fire Escape in central California. He was the one who had flown Wendy and me down to Southern California when our father had a stroke. Russ and Bruce didn't see one another often but the strong bond was evident.

I came home one day to find Russ sitting alone in the dark. Bruce had been killed instantly when his car was hit by a truck running a stop sign. Russ was very strong and certainly knew without any doubt he would see Bruce again someday. But those losses also chipped away at his emotions as our relationship was deteriorating. Russ had lost one of his few options for support or talking things over.

I suppose that's true for a lot of guys but I knew it was especially hard for Russ. We began to argue more frequently. Russ was doing a lot of work as an accountant whenever the group was not traveling. I misinterpreted his self-reliance and work ethic as evidence of his lack of interest. We began to talk about separating.

One of my personal issues was I found it difficult to understand and relate in certain social dynamics. I mentioned Toni earlier, a woman from Calvary Chapel who rented a room from us for a while. Toni worked in a facility for severely mentally disabled people. Apparently some people in the church looked with suspicion on my relationship with Toni long before it occurred to me to be concerned. Toni came out to me as a lesbian. But she didn't seem as "different" to me as she apparently did to some others. I'd seen Toni go through some tough times and be seriously misunderstood. Her confession of being a lesbian was not a big deal to me. I had friends who lived with someone before marrying them or who got pregnant before they were married.

She began to feel as different as people seemed to perceive her to be and finally asked to talk to me. We put blankets out in the sun and talked for a few hours. She told me she was on the volleyball team at the local junior college and felt funny around some of the women. I asked what kind of funny. After many allusions, which I missed, she finally told me she felt she was in love with another woman on the team. I was shocked, not at her revelation, but that it was so hard for her to tell me. I tried to sort of brush it off by replying everyone had feelings and it was only what you did with them that mattered.

She said, "No, you don't understand. If you're dating a guy and you're tempted to have sex with him you at least know that someday you'll be able to do that. But the feelings I have will never be right. I will never be fulfilled or feel connected to the person I'm in love with. I will just always be wrong." She wept openly.

I had a lot of compassion for Toni after what she told me. I understood her point. Neither of us even considered the idea that the teaching we'd had about homosexuality could be wrong or that there could be other interpretations of Scripture. But, somehow, I felt like I understood her pain. I didn't question why I resonated so much with her concerns. I loved Toni and her sense of humor and her passion for being right with Jesus. I didn't really think much more of it.

Later I saw Toni at an event where there were Ping-Pong and pool tables and dancing. We were both laughing at our lack of prowess at the games when Toni, still laughing, said, "Well, I can't say that I'm being persecuted for righteousness sake anymore." I was struck to the heart, and still am, that Toni felt so entirely disqualified from being right with God that she could only laugh it off. In her eyes, she was a joke to God. I had never seen anyone slip so visibly, quickly, and completely from the Body of Christ.

It became clear to me over the years many people at Calvary Chapel had wondered if Toni was gay and wondered if I had a sexual relationship with her. I did not. But I loved Toni and I had seen the years she spent poring over her Bible, inviting people to church and finding rides to get them there, caring for people who could not care for themselves and doing it for Jesus' sake. I still think of her today and admire her caring heart.

A pastor of a church that happens to welcome gay Christians was telling me recently the church shouldn't have to specifically say they welcome gay people. They said the church fails all kinds of people – people who are single sometimes feel left out, people with kids can't always participate in adult activities if childcare is not provided, people with especially difficult children may be left out entirely. People of different worship backgrounds or cultures or colors may feel unrepresented and so on. But, as Toni pointed out to me so long ago, the single person might feel there is hope to find a partner. The couples with kids may arrange childcare. But for most of the gay community, acceptance from the conservative or evangelical churches is simply not an option at all and they feel it never will be.

In many ways Toni's life mirrored the conflict Russ and I were going through. It often felt like we lived in two different worlds. Some people think we were being hypocritical to continue in ministry if we were troubled in other areas of our lives. That was never our intent. I didn't feel any of us "pretended" to believe what we said or faked an attitude for stage or audience. In fact, part of what kept us traveling and singing was we DID believe all we said and sang about. It was in this place we thought we were "putting God first," being unselfish, and offering help and hope to others. But our marriage was stressed on the road and at home.

I had other difficulties with life on the road. I had become accustomed to the idea I had to be able to fall asleep quickly in whatever time was available. Sleep had to fit in between my children's care, my turns to drive, time zone changes, and morning, afternoon, and/or evening concerts. One solution was a commonly prescribed drug called Valium. It was so common I remember a skit on Saturday Night Live where someone in an office says she's so stressed she needs a Valium, and every co-worker in the room holds out a bottle to her.

We had a family physician who prescribed large bottles of Valium with the idea each of us could use it as needed. I was the one who struggled with setting boundaries about using it. I was unaware of the problem it was creating for me for a long time. Whenever it was time for me to grab a nap, for instance if one of the kids had been up sick all night, but was now quieted down, I took a small handful of pills. I didn't realize how deeply I relied on them to quiet my mind.

Russ and I were traveling with the group in Toronto one weekend and singing at 100 Huntley Street (Canada's popular evangelical program). One of the women shared with me God had been giving her a wonderful daily worship time. She explained she'd always had a hard time and was feeling guilty about her daily prayer time. If she set an alarm, she woke up kids and dogs. If she tried to stay up late she fell asleep halfway through. She said she had really prayed about it and found one night she woke up about 3am, had a lovely prayer time, and went right back to sleep. She woke up refreshed the next morning. She smiled about how special it was to her that Jesus just quietly woke her up in the night to have time with her.

The very first thing I thought was, "Jesus *couldn't* wake me up at 3am."

That thought startled me. Of course I knew God could do anything but it showed me between surgeries and pain medication along with Valium, I was actually controlling my life with drugs. The pain meds had become less needed since my hysterectomy in 1978. I didn't want to be like my parents living my life from one mind-altering chemical to another. I determined I would try to stop taking them.

By the fall of 1979, Russ and I both admitted we had failed at counseling. After what seemed to me to be disasters with the styles of Christian counseling, our last counselor had made many specific instructions. Each of the instructions, we performed perfunctorily. There, check that one off the list. Unfortunately, the gap between us was greater than the list.

Finally, Russ told me he just could not give me the level of attention I needed. He felt overwhelmed with my neediness and honestly, I couldn't blame him. He suggested he could give me 5% of the attention I needed but I should look for 95% somewhere else. We confided in Ivy, our counselor at the time, this was how we felt. She finally suggested separation.

# 31
# ALCOHOLICS ANONYMOUS

We were home and Russ was working a temp job. I decided it was important to get off the medications. I couldn't think of anyone at church to speak to about it so I called the local phone number for Alcoholics Anonymous. I had plenty of experience with the family programs I had attended with my mother. Now legal drugs were running my life and I needed to get "clean."

Whoever he was, the man who answered the phone for AA was perfect for me. I explained to him I came from an alcoholic family and I was taking far too much Valium every day. "I can't seem to stop on my own," I confided. He immediately answered, "Oh down here we just call those Valium a very dry martini. Come on over to the Alano Club. There's a meeting at noon." He probably saved my life.

I went to the meeting. I didn't realize at every meeting someone reads parts of the book Alcoholics Anonymous aloud. I just knew when I went to my first meeting someone handed me a typewritten page of paper and said, "Would you read this please?" I sat dutifully and read it to myself and handed it back to him. He looked oddly at me and I assured him, "Oh I did read it." It was only later I realized he meant for me to read it aloud during the meeting.

As people went around the table sharing their stories and struggles, I was baffled by the references to "the Big Book." I assumed it was a reference to the Bible. You know, like the Big Man in the Sky or something. But the more that people quoted specific lines from the writing the more confused I became.

"Well, the Big Book says, 'we will be amazed before we are halfway through,'" or, "Like it says in the Big Book, we have to have rigorous honesty." I kept thinking, *"What translation could they possibly be referring to that they found that in the Bible?"*

By the time it got to be my turn to identify myself as a newcomer, the leader of the meeting encouraged me to share something. I really couldn't imagine what I could say until it suddenly came into focus for me I could say anything. I could share any pain, any shame I had and no one would react in horror Marsha Stevens said such a thing, or even, heaven forbid, used a bad word.

I know it sounds odd but I was so accustomed to being on stage or at least on display somewhere, I was amazed there was a place where I didn't have to look "good" to be accepted. I left the meeting and thought I couldn't really go home yet. I felt I needed more help and more time to be there to really make a commitment to stop using the drugs. I was so inexperienced in socializing or any sort of casual conversation. I went to my car and got my guitar so I could bring it back to the patio and sing. *That* I knew how to do! I sat and sang. Some people stopped to listen, clapped a bit or said they liked the lyrics and moved on to talk in groups. One woman hung back and listened to song after song.

Finally, she approached me. "Are you Marsha's sister?"
"Umm, nope. I'm Marsha. What's your name?"
"Winky."
Winky was visibly shaken when I said, "My name is Marsha and I assume I'm an addict."

The guy next to me said, "The Big Book says the only requirement for membership is a desire to stop drinking and using. You don't need to assume anything. You wanna stop drinking or using, you're in the right place." I stopped equivocating. I didn't want to be anything like my parents. I didn't want to abuse prescription drugs. I wanted to be clean and sober.

After group, Winky asked if I wanted to go out for coffee. She said she had heard me sing and loved all the groups that sang at Calvary Chapel. Then she surprised me by saying she was angry God allowed me to be an alcoholic or addict. I was stumped. I had never been angry with God but I was certain God was big enough to handle our human emotional ups and downs. Still, I wasn't sure why she was angry.

I have to be a little creative here in quoting Winky because she spoke very frankly and with many expletives: "I'm such a screw-up so of course I would be an alcoholic. But you're special and you've decided to serve God with your whole life. How could Jesus let you be an addict?" I knew she was serious but I laughed out loud. And I thought something I've thought many times in my Christian walk, *"If they only knew."*

People think when I say this, or when I wrote a song that said it, I had homosexuality in mind. I did not – either then, with Winky, or later when I wrote the song. I struggle with being human; falling, failing, doubting, hurting, and acting in anger or selfishness. I thought if Winky knew how deeply I was hurting, how much I wanted to be loved and understood, she would walk away surprised at how far I fell short. If she knew how alone I felt in my world, how futile my attempts were to meet even my own expectations, let alone those of all the people around me, she might not even want to stay and talk. Winky didn't walk away.

I began to go to meetings every day for a while, which was what my sponsor (a woman I'll call Ruth) told me I should do. I was uncomfortable with her expectations. She knew me through my music and sort of expected me to be what she would consider a perfect Christian. To her, I just needed to stop taking mind-altering medications or drugs. The first three steps of AA seemed pretty obvious to me. For those of you who don't know them, here they are:

## THE TWELVE STEPS OF ALCOHOLICS ANONYMOUS

1. *We admitted we were powerless over alcohol (include here whatever your addiction is)—that our lives had become unmanageable.*
2. *Came to believe that a Power greater than ourselves could*

*restore us to sanity.*

3. *Made a decision to turn our will and our lives over to the care of God as we understood Him.*
4. *Made a searching and fearless moral inventory of ourselves.*
5. *Admitted to God, to ourselves, and to another human being the exact nature of our wrongs.*
6. *Were entirely ready to have God remove all these defects of character.*
7. *Humbly asked Him to remove our shortcomings.*
8. *Made a list of all persons we had harmed, and became willing to make amends to them all.*
9. *Made direct amends to such people wherever possible, except when to do so would injure them or others.*
10. *Continued to take personal inventory and when we were wrong promptly admitted it.*
11. *Sought through prayer and meditation to improve our conscious contact with God, as we understood Him, praying only for knowledge of His will for us and the power to carry that out.*
12. *Having had a spiritual awakening as the result of these Steps, we tried to carry this message to alcoholics, and to practice these principles in all our affairs.*

Alcoholic Anonymous Publishing

Like a lot of Christians who encounter a need for the 12-step programs, I thought the first three steps were sort of a breeze. When I tried to say I thought the rest of the steps seemed daunting to me, Ruth suggested I read a book on how to be a Christian woman.

I have to say I don't respond well to anyone telling me "how" to be myself. I really wrestle with reading any self-help book except the Bible. I do enjoy reading biographies and autobiographies – stories of what other people have gone through and how they dealt with life. But anything that smacks of, "I am wise and know more than you do about how you should be, feel, and act in the world," pretty much causes an immediate rejection reaction in me. "Who are you to tell me how to be?"

The meetings were great and people there had mostly learned to tell their own accounts of their lives. There is no cross-talk in meetings so, no matter what I shared, no one started their sharing with, "Marsha, here's what you should do." The meetings became a lifeline for me as I realized I did need help to stop taking the pills.

This was 1979 and it was the beginning of some major changes which would last the rest of my life.

Ruth was increasingly not helpful. Someone might share a similar situation in their own life and how they felt they handled or mishandled it. All of those personal stories I found helpful. But Ruth seemed harsh and judgmental; she drew some pretty open conclusions about who was a "real Christian" in our 12-step groups.

It was a bad time for me. After my hysterectomy, I had been taking hormone replacements and I had to stop those as well as the painkillers. I was having hot flashes and night sweats. Along with those I also had the shakes so bad they were almost tremors. I could not control them no matter how much I tried. I had miserable headaches and nausea to the point I couldn't even think about ministry. I felt tense to the point of bursting.

People at the 12 step meetings had warned about these symptoms as well as the simple fact drugs had been burying my feelings. As I came off the drugs, all these emotions would tend to surface all at once. Members of the 12 step groups gave me phone numbers to call "any time day or night."

# 32
# WINKY

I took the AA phone lists home. I also ended up temporarily putting a phone extension in the garage. That way I wouldn't wake anyone when I got up at night and called someone. More and more often, that someone was my new friend Winky. She was very patient and full of words of wisdom. Later I found out she had these "words of wisdom" posted up on the wall facing her bed so, when other AA members called, she could look sleepily up and quote from them. Winky had several favorites.

"K.I.S.S: Keep it Simple Stupid" and "One Day at a Time," along with "There but for the Grace of God." "Just for today, I will not be in charge." She also had more spiritual comments like, "When Life Gets Too Hard to Stand, Kneel," "Let go and Let God," "Easy Does It," "This Too Shall Pass," along with perhaps a dozen more. A big part of her "wisdom" was putting up things to say to people who call you crying at 3am and want you to say something meaningful!
Winky was funny, too. She made me - and everyone else - laugh. She'd tell outrageous stories. People at get-togethers would look at her and say "Tell a joke about..." and pick topics, which she could always do. Toenails or toothbrushes, whatever the topic, she had a joke for it.

I began to go to meetings with her and afterward out with a circle of her friends. Winky had grown up being told she was retarded and had been taken out of school in second grade. She didn't learn to read until a couple of years before I met her. Now she was in college to get a degree and become certified as a psychiatric technician in California so she could work at Fairview State Hospital for the Developmentally Disabled.

At the time, Fairview housed almost 2,000 full time residents and had almost that many workers. I visited there and found the people never seen by most of us in society. While she was an aide, and later a psychiatric technician, all of the clients Winky was working with were considered to have an IQ of less than 10. They were people who could never dress, clean or feed themselves. There were people with disorders that seemed to me to be horrific. One man had a tongue that continued to grow throughout his life. Besides his profound mental disabilities, his tongue hung far outside of his mouth making any speech impossible and eating very difficult. From time to time he would bite his tongue, resulting in staggering wounds. Periodically, he would have surgery to shorten the length, but it kept growing.

Others in the unit had hydrocephalus that had been untreated or was untreatable and could not even lift their own heads. Several patients were so severe their skulls were three feet or more in circumference.

I was astounded anyone would choose to work there as a career. Winky took her own experience of being called "retarded" when she was young and turned it into a passion to help people. She had been taken out of school and pitied and she wanted to help them do all they could with their abilities.

Over the years she found several people who were actually not mentally disabled at all. One was an amazing pianist who had been committed by his parents early in the 1930s for "fooling around with a girl in the barn." He was functionally underdeveloped since he had been sitting and sleeping and eating in a room with poorly functioning people for almost 50 years when Winky met him. However, she found he had Parkinson's disease. With very little coaching and a change in his medication regimen he was able to play piano again. He also relearned his communication and reading skills.

Another woman was found to simply be suffering with cerebral palsy. She had no other deficits. Once Winky determined this, the woman was quickly placed in an appropriate home to continue her learning. Ultimately, Winky's groups had far more out-placements than any other workers or psych-techs that worked at the hospital.

When the hospital hired two new psychiatrists on staff, they were sent first to Winky's group to see what happened when just one person decided to treat all the clients as though they were just like she was when she was a child. Most continued to need some treatment but all of them became far higher functioning than they had ever been.

Around this time, I started having some difficulty with my vision. This was especially evident with reading any material. I did not know at the time it was caused by the drug withdrawals. The women at the Calvary Chapel women's group had been praying about it with me. Kay Smith, Pastor Chuck's wife, led the women's group and asked to have lunch with me after the group time. I was ecstatic. Lunch alone with Kay Smith! I couldn't believe she wanted to spend time with me. *Maybe I'd made it into the inner circle at last.*

I learned a new song on the guitar to sing for her and waited outside in the Calvary Chapel parking lot for her to meet me for lunch. When she came out, she was with the psychiatrist's wife (someone who seemed to share a lot about other people at church). I was horrified. I *won't be sharing anything personal during this luncheon,* I thought. I never did sing the song for her.

They were ready to go and I hopped in the back seat. I listened to them talking about the purse/handbag sale at Nordstrom that weekend and felt my heart sink. *I would never be a part of their group of friends.* My $2 Goodwill leather bag was slung over my shoulder.

At lunch, after some awkward conversation, Kay told me she would be willing to get me the King James Bible on cassette to help me cope with my vision problems. I told her I was praying and I thought my vision was improving. Finally, she asked if I thought there wasn't a "work of the enemy" going on in my life.

I have to say again my first reaction to anything actually being demonic is a sort of relief. I mean, we have victory over the enemy. That's a clear-cut thing. The late C.S. Lewis wrote sin is often divided into three "types." He called it the World, the Flesh, and the Devil.

The world is...complicated. Praying for the world often feels to me like praying for my team to win. You would never pray that, right? Because who knows if that's really God's will? So if "the World" is part of a problem, I consider it sticky.

Then, "the Flesh," that was something else. I mean even the apostle Paul said, in Romans 7: 19-24: "The things I want to do, I don't do and the things I DO want to do, I fail to do...wretched man that I am..." So of course, I feel like it's hard for me to understand what things in my own "flesh" I need to handle myself, and what I just have to turn over to the Lord. I mean, I don't eat a half-gallon of ice cream every day and then pray to lose weight.

But the Devil – that's a done deal. So if something is "of the enemy" or "from the devil," I'm all set. Let's pray, cast it out and be done with it. That victory has already been won! But for some reason, the two women were not eager to just "pray and bind the enemy in Jesus' name." Kay hemmed and hawed and finally got to her question. "Did you and Toni ever have a sexual relationship or attraction while she lived with you?"

Nothing of the sort had ever entered my mind. I was aghast. *Toni was my friend, period. Even if Kay was concerned about this, how could she have this conversation with someone else here?* Once more, how did I explain myself without sounding like a "lady who doth protest too much," as Shakespeare put it? At any rate, there were rumors going around church I was gay long before I ever knew about it. I explained Toni and I were friends and that's the end of the story. I left the lunch despondent. Those feelings continued to plague me even as Russ and I continued to talk about separation.

Since Russ and I argued a lot, I knew it was hard on the kids. But I didn't know either how to explain it or to stop it. I avoided the problem by spending more time over at Winky's house.
One afternoon at her house, I said I was struggling with what Jesus expected of me. She put on a record. You remember those, right,

the big round black vinyl discs with a hole in the middle? It was the Blackwood Brothers singing, "He is Here Right Now." It was meant to comfort me, but one of the lines was, "you don't need to wait; you don't need to beg," I thought, *"That isn't true. I have waited and I have begged and I'm still hurting."*

I thought about Winky and I realized I had somehow both strong and familiar feelings for her. I tried to think of other times I had felt this way and realized with a start that, although it had not been anyone in particular I had thought about, the only times I had experienced this strong emotional attachment was to another woman or girl. I rolled that thought around in my head. Could I be in love with Winky? I knew I was.

I hated feeling that way. Nothing about it could ever work out. I had to smash the feelings. But the more I thought about my reactions over the years, the clearer it became; the crushes on summer camp counselors' year after year, the infatuation with women who were my teachers and the long loving letters I had written to them, the slumber parties where other girls waited for boys to crash the party and I waited for the first girl to cry (there was always a girl who cried at a slumber party - then I could be the one to hold her in my arms without defending my actions,) the practice-kisses-for-boys that I rehearsed with Allison in 6th grade. The thoughts came crashing in on me. Could I be one of *them*? Was that library book I read in my early teens right? Was I having homosexual feelings?

I immediately began to pray to die. I would never hurt my family, kids, or friends by doing anything obvious to kill myself. However, I prayed hard and reasoned with God if I died, everyone could just go through the mourning process and move on. They'd never have to be disillusioned about how bad I was or know I had gay feelings. I thought about going back to controlling my emotions with medications but I'd come too far to try that again. It had obviously affected my health. Russ and I had talked a lot with counselors about how much "attention" it seemed I needed (something I felt almost as bad about as I did at the thought of being gay), and about separating and we did separate at the end of that year.

Talking to the rest of my family was a very different experience. Each person had singular reactions. My mother had remarried after my father died and she chose a wonderful man whom my kids called Grampy Bill. I hand-wrote a 32-page letter trying to explain my "gay feelings for Winky" to my mother and Bill. People actually did stuff like that in the 70s. I waited for my letter to arrive and called my mom. I was baffled when the first thing she said was, "Well, I'm certainly going to miss the grandchildren." I never did find out what she meant by that – whether she was not going to see me with my children, or if she thought Russ would take our children, or if she was planning never to see me again.

But Bill's reaction was overwhelmingly loving. "Oh honey," he exclaimed, "that's wonderful news. Here I thought you weren't going to have anyone to love you and you have Winky. That's great!"

My sister had deeper and clearer reservations. Apparently she had heard about times Winky's car was in my driveway and had surmised we had been having a sexual relationship all along. We hadn't but that was really a moot point now. She knew Russ and I had been falling apart for a while but she believed strongly I was wrong and that nothing to do with homosexuality could ever be right.

Winky's friends were not so troubled about the issue of homosexuality as they were about her being involved at all during her first year of sobriety and especially of being involved with me when I had only weeks of being clean.

Pete Jacobs had already stopped traveling with Children of the Day, but I was still close to him and to his wife, Hanneke. She told me that she had been praying for me a few weeks earlier and God had revealed to her I was gay.

Then, there was Chuck Smith. He was adamant and absolute, and so over-the-top in my mind. He spoke with conviction and a tinge of condemnation, not solely for me, but for Russ, too. "I've known for almost a year now you were gay. But if Russ wasn't man enough to meet your needs then you could have divorced him and married someone else.  Everyone would have forgotten all about (it)."

I was stunned.  There were so many things wrong, and troubling, about that statement I could barely respond at all. Russ being "man enough" was completely wrong and had nothing to do with it. By our church's teaching divorce was clearly taught as being at least as wrong as homosexuality so how would divorce have been ok? It was demeaning and unfair to talk about Russ that way. I hated that.

But most of all, again, that question: *How did people know I was gay before I did?* How is that possible? Doesn't that automatically mean "gay" is something you are, not something you do? And how ironic was it the very people most convinced homosexuality was a sin were the ones telling me it wasn't a feeling, but an identity?

Later, Papa Chuck would have more talks with me about that and I could feel his brokenness on the subject, especially when he once said to me, "You cannot tell me they don't recruit!" There was so much pain and bitterness in his tone and my heart went out to him, but I never did learn where that pain came from for him.

On December 31, 1979, Russ moved out and Winky moved in. As far as the rest of my world was concerned, Russ and I had been fine until I "turned gay."

# 33
# DIVORCE, LOSS, AND CUSTODY

Several times, Russ and I had talked about getting back together. I don't know that anyone is really ready for a divorce but we were so unprepared. We didn't know others who'd been divorced and I certainly had moments of panic that I couldn't go through it. It seemed to me both of us had minimized the impact on the kids. They were just about age 5 and 7 when we separated. But so often we had traveled separately, or had them at Marilyn and Karen's home, or spending nights elsewhere, it didn't seem like it would be that awful. As long as we let them know we both loved them it would be fine, we assumed. We were very wrong.

One day Russ missed a visit with the kids – no big deal, just a minor change of plans. I got up to find that 5-year-old Johnny had left the house. We hunted all over and went door to door looking for him. Hours later, when I finally found him a few blocks away, he said he was afraid if he went to school he'd get in trouble and not be able to see his Dad. I was heartbroken and told him he would always be able to see Russ.

Just at this same time, tennis player Billie Jean King was starting to be outed as a lesbian. One of the first things her husband Larry did was to say it was partly his fault and he would rekindle their marriage. That didn't work out as I think everyone knows by now but, at the time, I had begged for that. At least Russ had the foresight to avoid that kind of futility.

Besides, in our limited theology he sort of had the golden ticket. The only reason you could get divorced and not be judged sinful by the church was if your spouse was unfaithful. He left our marriage with grace and, I think, with some relief. It was the beginning of 1980 and he remarried in 1981 to the woman to whom he is still married over thirty-five years later.

I called Pat, my high school boyfriend, who was now a divorced single parent. He drove the 2 ½ hours to see me. I told him the church seemed to me to be saying a guy, a man, really any male would be more acceptable to them than me being gay or being in love with a woman. We visited for two days and had some long, tender talks. But it all only left both of us knowing the people in church who had "known" I was a lesbian, were right.

Winky and I floundered in our own ways. Both of us were broken. Both of us were barely in "recovery." And both of us were in love. My sponsor, Ruth, promptly dropped me and said she could never sponsor anyone who was gay. This was only the beginning of being excluded for being gay.

Winky had two kids of her own. Penny was just shy of her 14th birthday, and Maury was 16. Penny was a big hit with my kids. Naomi loved having a cool older girl in the house. Penny babysat for her and Johnny from time to time. Winky's kids were in public school, mine were in Christian schools. Naomi went to school at Calvary Chapel. A few weeks after Winky moved in someone at Calvary school told the school I should no longer be allowed to pick up my kids at school and Chuck should investigate whether Naomi was being molested.

Naturally he called Naomi into his office right away. She confirmed she had told a friend she had a secret. She and Penny would play games under the sheets after they were supposed to be in bed and she didn't want to get in trouble. But when Chuck asked her what games they were she said it was usually Chinese checkers but sometimes regular checkers.

I tried to understand people were just uninformed and not trying to be cruel or judgmental with their suspicions. But it got worse when Penny began to have one angry outburst after another with her mother and brother. Winky tried giving Penny a break by letting her visit an aunt for a while to let things cool off.

When Penny came home, we tried to run a much tighter ship. One rule was if you were too sick to wake up early for school then you had to get up and go to the doctor. One-day Penny was washing out the sink when she suddenly complained of chest pain. It was such an odd complaint for a 14-year-old that we were immediately concerned. Later, she said it went away and she leaned her breastbone against the sink while she was cleaning it and thought it was a bruise.

We would never have remembered the event but the next Tuesday, Penny said she felt too sick to go to school. She just felt…crummy. I got her up and took her to the HMO clinic with her insurance card. We saw a doctor we'd never seen before. I thought she seemed pretty thorough for someone who was just treating a teenager with malaise (medical speak for "feeling crummy"). She drew blood, tested for mononucleosis, which was negative. They told her to drink plenty of fluid and get some rest. Come back in two days if she didn't feel better.

Sure enough, by Thursday Penny still felt too sick for school. Winky and I talked to people to see if there were big tests going on and asked Maury and her friends if she had a problem with a friend or a boyfriend. I also took her back to the doctor Thursday morning. This time the doctor did more testing, including another blood draw for hepatitis. The doctor decided to put Penny on antibiotics even though she had no specific infection but had no other ideas.

The other rule we had about missing school was if you were too sick to go to school on a Friday you would not be allowed to run around with friends over the weekend. Friday morning Penny got herself up to school. Winky and I relaxed. It must have been teenage angst over something we didn't know. That night we let her stay over at a friend's house.

At 2 am the phone woke us up. We were not immediately panicked since people did call from AA at that hour. Winky took the phone but in the quiet of the night I could hear a woman saying we needed to get to Hoag Hospital immediately. She would not give any more information on the phone. We woke Maury to let him know to watch my little ones and drove in numb silence to the hospital.

They took us to a private office and a brutally cavalier doctor walked in. He had blood spatters on his white coat and the very first thing he said was, "Well, it looks like we have a dead teenager on our hands. What kind of drugs was she on?"

I was nearly as angry as I was anguished. Winky asked if she could see Penny. The doctor, looking at his messy coat, said, "Well just so you are aware we're still working on her in there." Somehow this seemed to combine with our mutual denial to indicate Penny was still alive, being "worked on." It sounded like there was hope. But when Winky went to the bed behind the drawn curtain, Penny was completely alone, cold, naked, full of IV lines, intubated, and clearly already dead. The hard reality started sinking in.

Winky's pain was indescribable. There were days I could hear her wails from inside the house when I just pulled into the driveway. Her AA friends did all they could to be with her every moment. To them, I was still a sort of intruder who had come into their friend's life more recently than they had and their biggest concern was for Winky's sobriety surviving her loss.

Winky felt compelled to find out why Penny had died and why they kept saying it was drugs. After all we'd been through so much with Penny we felt certain she was not on drugs. I finally went to the police station myself and asked a detective to tell me why they kept calling it an overdose. He explained young teenagers with no other physical ailments were presumed to have died from drugs and said it took a lot of time to test for every single drug it might be. "Besides," he said, "she had track marks." Starting with that detective, I spent weeks trying to get it clarified and proven with physician records, that those were not track marks. She died on Friday night. She'd had blood tests drawn on Tuesday and Thursday that week. Six weeks after her death, the "track marks" notes were still on her documents at the coroner's office where cause of death had yet to be determined.

Penny's funeral was unbearable. It was all Winky could do to get through it. It was impossible for me to be with her. I went up to sing and her mother and sisters moved into my place to be sure I could not sit with her after I sang. Her AA friends took her home with them afterward. I had my own kids to care for and Winky had Maury, a 16-year-old only child now with no one who understood him and his pain.

All of that was difficult enough but then I began to hear from people who said this was God's judgment on our family for the sin of homosexuality. I was dumbfounded. What God did they serve? I began to separate myself from people who could believe anything like that. In the meantime, Russ and I navigated our divorce proceedings and tried to keep things as uneventful as possible. Our biggest conflicts were just ahead with the custody hearing, which took place not long after.

I chose an attorney I knew would be sympathetic to me as a woman who was in a relationship with another woman. This man was known in the gay community as an advocate to the cause but he did not know me. He also did not take the time to get to know me.

Russ's attorney, on the other hand, was very well prepared. He was from Calvary Chapel and was, naturally, sympathetic to Russ' cause. After reading the initial settlement paperwork, I thought the process would be pretty cut and dried. California was, and is, a community property state and I thought we would just divide our possessions evenly and then work out a custody agreement in which Russ would get to visit our children often.

However, by then Russ had come to the belief my homosexuality was dangerous to our children. I'm sure Russ would never have said God killed Penny to punish Winky and me for our sexuality. But many people in the church had spoken to him about the danger of allowing the children to stay with me. He had come to feel somehow our behavior had contributed to Penny's death. His belief was something along the lines that our own personal immorality had led to a home where immorality was accepted. He concluded that was why Penny got into the immorality of drug use, which killed her.

We were required to put our children into counseling, in which Russ and I both participated. This turned out to be problematic at best. One counselor asked our daughter Naomi, who was seven years old, "If Mama bird lives in one tree and Daddy bird lives in another tree where does the baby bird go?" Naomi would just say, "To the tree."

The counselor would not give up: "Well, which tree does the baby bird go to, the Mommy's tree or the Daddy's tree?" Again Naomi responded, "To the tree." She was not fooled and was determined, even as a child, to not choose between her mommy and her daddy.

The court appointed psychologist was also concerned about Penny's presumed drug use and what caused her death. Just before the court case I finally went to the coroner's office and explained how not knowing the cause of death was likely to affect my hearing. I finally found a listening ear. I knew Penny was not on drugs but I couldn't prove it. Penny's body had been cremated but the coroner had kept blood and specimens of various organs for further study.

When the coroner herself finally talked to me, she understood and began testing for something other than drugs. As soon as she looked at Penny's x-rays and at her heart muscle she saw what everyone had missed. The illness Penny had been suffering with had been the flu and the virus had gone to her heart. The coroner identified the virus, which had completely overwhelmed Penny's heart tissue. She had died of viral myocarditis and would likely have needed a heart transplant even if it had been caught earlier. It was not actually hard to find but no one had been looking. We got the findings just as I went to court with Russ.

Regarding our music, I assumed any songs I had written before our marriage would belong to me just as any Russ had written would be his. This turned out to be a wrong assumption. I signed the papers, encouraged to do so by my attorney only to discover all our music would be jointly owned. For this reason, Russ sometimes was credited as a co-writer of "For Those Tears I Died" even though I wrote it before I ever knew him.

My attorney had no understanding of copyright law as it pertained to musical compositions. He did ask the judge about the issue but the judge responded with, basically, "I will hear your arguments if you want, but I am 99.9% certain I will rule the material is owned 50–50. This is a community property state and I'm not going to hear anything about exceptions for music."

It turned out that Russ's position was the song had increased in value during our marriage and all the work he did with Children of the Day was part of that increase in value. I disagreed with that position but I knew all the hours Russ spent doing the bookkeeping for the group was seriously underappreciated. In later years, Russ and I came to a different agreement on royalties.

My first priority was the custody issue so I was not inclined to go to battle over the music issue. I was distressed by the judge's flippant attitude but my kids' welfare was far more important. During the hearing Russ's attorney asked me a series of questions designed to leave a specific impression. I felt he was trying to corner me but I wasn't sure what he was going for. At one point, he asked whether a pay stub he held out was my "last" one. I did some temp work and didn't know if it was my most recent so I tried to state that. He insisted I answer only with a yes or a no. He asked me if the last time Russ had visited there were children's clothes "all over the living room." The answer was yes as I was sorting laundry at the time. But I was not allowed to explain, because the attorney immediately asked the judge to admonish me to answer solely with a "yes" or a "no." I was sternly warned. Then the bombshell came.

He asked if I had been hospitalized in a psychiatric hospital for two weeks in June of 1972. He demanded, "and answer only with a yes or no!" I said, "Yes." I couldn't say it was right after my father died or that it was a voluntary hospitalization for depression. Then he asked me, "Yes or no, Mrs. Stevens, is it true you were hospitalized SEVEN more times in the following 5 years?"

I had experienced seven additional hospitalizations in the few years after that. I had to answer "yes." I was not permitted to explain the subsequent hospitalizations were not in a psychiatric hospital but were for multiple large ovarian cysts, which were treated at the time by surgical removal. The surgeries had removed the cysts and saved my ovaries until I could have my two children. Then I had gone back for a hysterectomy, which removed the ovaries. Everyone in the courtroom was led to believe I had returned to the psychiatric hospital seven more times.

I assumed my attorney would set the record straight but he seemed to have forgotten the information I had given him. He stood and asked, "Didn't you have a miscarriage one of those times?" I had to say, "No," to that and leave the misimpression.

The judge hearing our case was not actually a sitting judge but an attorney who was acting "pro tem," or temporarily. This was significant because he did not particularly care whether his rulings would be overturned by a higher court. Noting the counselors had stated both Russ and I were good parents he awarded custody to Russ. He said, "Mom has never worked outside the home, (since I had no income showing) so let's give her a chance to see what that's like." He also issued a ruling, forbidding either one of us from speaking to our children about our views on homosexuality, whatever they might be. He added neither of us could live with anyone to whom we were not married or related by blood if we ever wanted to see our children.

In most cases, it does not look good for a judge to have one decision after another overturned in a superior court, but with an attorney who's just "playing" judge for the day, even that concern was obviated. He could say whatever he wanted. The court record reflected that as he closed by saying, "That might be a tough ruling to uphold but you'll have to get a date in superior court to change it, won't you."

The next available date in superior court was over two years away. For years I would physically shake if I drove through downtown

Santa Ana, where the hearing took place. I felt as though an omnipotence lingered there that very few people knew about. It could change your life on a whim.

Winky and I were forced to make some changes almost immediately. First, Winky and I had to vacate the home we had been sharing and find separate accommodations. This was part of the court requirements for being able to have visitation with my kids. When she had received word her daughter Penny had died it almost destroyed her. Now, at least she knew it was not from drugs. But I worried that our separation would drive her back into depression.

We had shared so much over the past year and were very close. Now, Winky had rented her own apartment. I needed to comply with the court ruling in order to be part of my children's lives. Neither of us were totally happy with the situation, but we would make it work.

# 34
# ON MY OWN

Even though Russ and I both worked for the same band for the same number of years I had no record of being paid (due to the 'biblical' policy of my husband receiving my pay). The judge declared I had "never worked outside the home," so I must find a job. I decided it needed to be something that could be a career so the judge would see I could support the kids. I went to the local junior college and completed the certification process for medical office assisting.

I quickly found a job at a Worker's Compensation clinic as a medical assistant. This was really my first permanent job outside of the music industry. I assisted with physicals and other minor issues. During my first couple of weeks working there a patient came in so critically ill I went to the doctor to alert him immediately. He brushed me off, so I called for an ambulance. I later got a letter from the patient who somehow tracked me down to thank me for saving his life. Unfortunately, I also got fired, let go for refusing to wait until the doctor "had time."

I told God, "This is just not fair. I did what I was supposed to do. How could you expect me to behave differently? It's absolutely not right." I felt abandoned. It was my first experience with feeling angry with God. In the past, I'd found reasons to question myself and see how I could have done things differently but not so with this situation.

That Friday afternoon, I went to get the list of available apartments from the rental agency quickly before anyone knew that I didn't have a job. The woman there told me there was nothing in my price range where the owners would allow more than one child, even for visitation periods. In my frustration I screamed at the woman who was supposed to be finding me a place to live. Then I sat in my car alone and just sobbed.

Finally, I got to the point where I was able to realize this was not how I needed to face life. I either had to trust God or I didn't. I returned to the woman at the rental agency at whom I had screamed and apologized for being rude and so awful to her. I explained I was going through a custody battle and had other tough things going on in my life. I said, "I took it out on you and it was completely inappropriate. I'm so very sorry."

She responded by saying she did have one listing for a certain client who was not on the regular print out. He was very particular about the kind of person he was willing to rent to. He wanted someone professional who was not prone to partying. She said, actually, kids were okay, but he wanted her to screen the potential renters for him. She continued, "Since you came back and apologized, I'm thinking you're probably the kind of person who is serious about your work and have a good perspective on life. So I'm going to call him to see if he'll show you the place."

I sighed deeply. "Thank you." I whispered.

The apartment was built on to the owner's garage at the back of his house. It was dilapidated and seemed sort of slapped together. It even had holes in some of the floorboards through which you could see the ground. But it had three bedrooms and everything else I needed. He allowed me to postpone paying the security deposit and move right in. He never raised the rent the whole seven years I wound up living there in Costa Mesa. What a blessing it turned out to be!

The very next Monday morning, I got a phone call, based on an ad I had responded to a few weeks earlier, offering me a job at a doctor's office.

Two weeks later, the police raided the Worker's Comp clinic where I had been fired. The "doctor" who had been so unprofessional with me was not even a real physician and was distributing drugs from the clinic. Because my time at the clinic had been so brief I was

spared even an interrogation. I flew completely under the radar.
The other employees had their lives disrupted by the intensive investigation. They had to testify in court and some of them were even charged with complicity in the drug sales. The "doctor" was incarcerated and I have heard his name mentioned on television shows about crime several times since then. In following years, I would find some of his reports in patient's charts. These patients had ongoing treatment based on that phony doctor. There was endless work to be done to discern what had really gone on with these patients.

God used my firing to spare me from all that. I have thought of that experience a thousand times since then. Pretty much the moment I look at a situation I think, "What is going on here, Lord?"
I stop and remember how grace-filled Jesus' plans for me really are. I can't imagine the faith of many of the people in the Bible. Mary, whatever her age, was surely very young when the angel spoke to her. What kept her going and believing for thirty-three years before she saw the promises fulfilled? Or, as Mark Lowry says, couldn't Gabriel have spared just one minute to tell Mary what was going on?

Others even accepted that the miracles God promised to them would come, but not in their lifetime. I'm grateful that Jesus knows my frailties and is always patient enough to remind me that His promises are true. Sometimes I need to be reminded a lot. The incident also gave me to fortitude to go back to school and earn my license as a registered nurse.

# 35
# RENEGOTIATING CUSTODY OF MY KIDS

Eventually, I turned my attention to appealing the custody situation. My mother and stepfather loaned me enough funds to pay for an attorney who would be more effective on my behalf. One of the downsides of this process was the attorney felt he had to "turn the tables" on Russ's attorney during the initial depositions.

He wanted to suggest Russ's relationship with his new wife had begun inappropriately while he was still married to me or Russ was in some way less than caring for the kids. I felt terrible as I listened to his line of questioning. Just as had been the case with me, Russ was forced to answer "yes" or "no" so the court reading the depositions would get the impression of some wrongdoing.

My attorney refused to consider any arguments from Russ's lawyer that referenced Scripture in any way. I think Russ's lawyer thought scripturally based arguments might have an impact on the proceedings now outside of a courtroom. We proceeded with an arbitrator according to California law and we were spared having to debate the meaning of Scripture as it relates to homosexuality.

I was actually glad Russ had found his new wife. Neither one of us had the intention of ruining the other's life. The arbitrator asked Russ and me to consider going to a counselor together with our children to discuss how best to proceed as parents. We all wanted the best possible situation for our children to grow into well-adjusted adults. My attorney disapproved and made sure at the very least, that nothing we discussed or revealed or decided in counseling could be used against either of us in court.

Russ agreed but, surprisingly, put in the agreement that the counselor could not be a Christian. I stated I wanted someone who shared our common faith and would seek God's guidance with us. I thought about the first verse in the first Psalm about walking "not in the counsel of the ungodly." Russ told me that his concern was for me to be comfortable and he thought I might feel judged by a Christian counselor. In the end, we settled on someone who shared our faith in Christ.

Each of us first met alone with the counselor. I shared with him the concern Russ perceived (and with which I agreed) that I needed excessive attention. The counselor asked me why this was an issue. I was actually shocked as I pondered the question. I assumed it was just a generally bad thing. The shock for me was not that I found I needed less attention than Russ felt I did but that my role might be to just accept that as part of who I am. I really considered needing attention sort of inherently "wrong." I could hear my grade school teachers decrying someone as "an attention-getter." I wasn't sure if I could accept that quality about myself. I worked so hard to be "acceptable" and perfect in how I projected myself to others.

On the other hand, the counselor disagreed with my understanding of the Scripture as it regards sexual orientation. But his point in interviewing us for so many hours, both together and separately, was to be sure of the best environment for the kids. We waited for his non-binding recommendation to our attorneys. In his 'findings letter' the first thing the counselor stated was that I "struggled with homosexuality," which impacted my ability to be a good parent. I hardly dared turn the page to see the rest.

However, it turned out that he recommended joint custody, with Johnny living with Russ and seeing me every other weekend and every Wednesday. He felt Naomi should reside with me. She would see Russ on a similar schedule. He felt each child was more closely bonded with their same-sex parent than with their sibling. The counselor felt having Johnny and Naomi together every weekend would allow the bonding they needed with one another. Many times I felt I had not "fought for Johnny" hard enough. But I don't think either Russ or I thought of this as a win/lose situation.

We agreed to the arrangement and lawyers detailed such specifics as where the children would spend major holidays and birthdays and so forth. We did not revisit the property settlement issues; however, we did decide to sell the house.

Naomi moved into my little place with me and quickly perceived she should not share details of my relationship with Winky with anyone. Naomi was eight at this time and had always deeply loved Winky. Johnny began his visits as well. Times with the kids went well. I loved having them back in my life on a regular basis. The thing that shocked me at the time was the freedom of sending the kids to Russ' every other weekend. Don't misunderstand. I love time with my kids. But young parents have so little time to work on any problems that arise. I wondered how many relationships might survive if they had every other weekend just to themselves.

At the time, the only other gay Christian Winky and I really knew was a Catholic priest. He was gay and celibate and I could openly discuss our issues with him. After the custody case, I spoke to him about how torn I was even about splitting up the kids in the agreement. He shocked me by saying, "Marsha, you've been a Christian long enough to know that you reap what you sow." I was hurt, wondering how he could say this to me when I was going through a divorce and I had been living without my children. Before I could frame a response he continued, "and the only thing you can do about that is to sow well today."

He was advising me to live in the present and not dwell on the pain of the past. He was right. I had been hiding, even from myself. I had used drugs to control my life for a time. It made me realize my job was to focus on building healthy relationships and being the best parent I could be now.

# 36
# RENEGOTIATING CUSTODY OF
# MY HEART

My relationship with the body of Christ had been wounded during the divorce and custody proceedings. I had gone through my first anger with God, been judged and misunderstood by my friends at church, and I had drawn away from the intensity and excitement of worship. I somehow thought I could walk away from church and just have a sort of private relationship with Jesus. But I longed for fellowship and sharing stories and praising God with other believers.

Finally, I went to a movie in theaters at the time. It was simply called Jesus. I went alone as though I didn't want the lightning to strike anyone else on the way to me. Although I knew the movie story was taken right from the book of Luke I somehow felt maybe the movie would make me feel guilty enough to not be gay anymore. I know that doesn't make any sense. But I had heard people so many times saying things like, "Be careful if you pray for patience; God will just give you more trials." Or, "If you hate bugs and snakes, God will make you a missionary to Africa."

Those ideas are ridiculously opposite of my actual experience in following Christ but, somehow, an angry or vindictive God is an easy lie to believe. Instead, as the movie started, I began to hear again those wonderful words and see the actions with which I was so familiar. My heart broke. *I love this Man. I worship him as Lord of my life. I want to be just like Him. When had I forgotten that? How could I have let that love and comfort be taken from me?*

The next day, I went to a huge Calvary Chapel beach baptism where I thought I could mingle anonymously. As I walked on the beach and listened to the worship, I thought, *"This is exactly what I think. This is exactly what I believe. This is exactly what I feel. I know how much Jesus gave for me and how much He loves me. When did I forget that?" I sank to my knees in the sand and prayed, "I don't know how I forgot You really love me. Somewhere along the line I started thinking it would be better for me to die and I hoped someday soon I could just get killed in an accident or something. But I want to be Yours - take me, lead me, make me completely Yours. In the meantime, let me be loving and unselfish. I really do want to be whoever You want me to be. Strike me straight if You want me to be straight. Just make me Yours no matter what. In Jesus' Name."*

I left there with an incredible sense of peace. I remembered I am not my own, I am bought with a price and I am none of my business anymore. I am not my problem, I'm God's problem and I trust God to continue a good work in me. I have had so many people in recent years tell me they're afraid to rededicate their hearts to Jesus because Jesus might take away the man or woman whom they love. My answer is always the same: He might. You still have to do it. You have to give up your plans and know God's plan for you is the best one there is. I realized that day the God of the universe could cause me to wake up and suddenly have blue eyes or be left-handed or five-foot-two. But I think God probably got it right the first time, and I'm going to continue to be a green-eyed, right-handed, five-foot-nine lesbian.

When I arrived home after my encounter with God on the beach, I found a letter from the counselor who had written to our attorneys about our custody issues. It was a personal letter to me. In his letter he said he felt he owed me an apology. He wasn't sure what he needed to apologize for specifically but he said, "I think my recommendation about custody is right. But, everywhere I go I meet someone who says you led them to the Lord. Every time I turn on the radio a song you have written is playing. God has not let up on me. In six months I have not heard anything but that you are a participant in the things of God." He said he knew the things he wrote in his legal opinion were negatively skewed.

He said he wasn't sure exactly why those things were wrong but he knew they were wrong. He did think his custody recommendations were sound. He would continue to study the matter, but in the meantime, he said he had to tell me he knew I was a fellow believer. I took his comments as God's way of answering my prayer on the beach, assuring me I still belonged to Christ.

I began taking the kids to Calvary Chapel Sunday School. I would often drop them off and worship elsewhere then return to pick them up. This practice was not at all acceptable at Calvary but the kids had friends there and I needed to worship somewhere I could feel accepted and welcomed. I kept searching for a church that could offer more than tolerance for my attendance.

I spent a lot of time on my own in the Scripture and also sneaked into the Fuller Seminary or other libraries trying to find out what the Bible actually said about sexual orientation. I focused on Scriptures that are commonly quoted as defining homosexuality as a sin. I struggled through Greek interlinear (Bibles that have the Greek words in between the English translated lines), and Hebrew language discussions.

I'm a long, long way from being a Biblical scholar but I was very surprised at how little mention of homosexuality is in the Bible. Only a handful of verses are assumed to be discussing LGBTQ people but there are 356 verses against sexual sins by heterosexuals (someone pointed out to me later those heterosexuals seem to need a lot more guidance and advice than homosexuals).

Sodom and Gomorrah was the first place I looked. I was actually shocked anyone thought this referred to homosexuality. All the men of Sodom wanted to rape the angels and Lot was going to let them rape his daughters to death instead? That's like thinking all of the guys in prison are gay because they rape a newcomer. That behavior is violence and power and control. I cannot imagine anyone reading a true homosexual orientation into that. It certainly is not discussing loving, same-sex couples.

Then I headed to Leviticus for the famous "man shall not lay with man as with a woman" rule. I understood some of the other rules for sexual contact. For instance, a woman being "unclean" and therefore untouchable for seven days after her cycle ended meant that she was available to her husband during the most potentially fertile part of her cycle. I felt pulling this one rule, about "men lying with men," out of so many other rules that we dismissed, was odd. That verse is Leviticus 20:13 and seen by conservatives as applying to people today but Leviticus 20:10 (just 3 sentences earlier) says adulterers should be executed. I won't belabor all the ones we clearly do NOT follow, but you get the point.

I also went to my concordance, and looked up "abominations." Shoot, the Torah is full of them. Well over 100. Mostly about animals we shouldn't eat. There was no Bible-on-search-engine yet! But my favorite "abomination" Scripture was from Proverbs 6:16-19. It is a list of "six things the Lord hates, seven which are an abomination unto God." It names "a proud look, a lying tongue, and hands that shed innocent blood, a heart that devises wicked imaginations, feet that be swift in running to mischief, a false witness that speaks lies." However, the last is the best, "Anyone who sows division among the brethren."

I read about David having a "love that is better than that of a woman" for Jonathan and they did do a lot of weird sneaking around behind their families' backs and kissing and hugging and declaring their love, but I was unconvinced. David is hardly the poster boy for anything to do with family values, anyway. Nathan the prophet called David out on the sins about which we read the most - David's adultery with Bathsheba and David essentially murdering her husband Uriah. But apparently at the time, no one thought it was weird to have numerous wives, or for David to want a "young girl to keep him warm in bed at night" when he got old.

Ruth and Naomi seemed lovely and I have since used Ruth's beautiful words to Naomi in speaking and songs. However, their lives and family structures are too different for me to compare to our culture and in the context of having to marry your brother-in-law if your husband dies, and so on. People don't seem to realize how many Bible teachings are not followed today since our entire culture and family structures are so entirely different.

The King James Version of the Bible, which was the one I first learned to study, never actually uses the word "homosexual" in it. The word really didn't exist in any Bible in the world before 1946, and I read a dozen or more different explanations of what the Greek and Arabic words and concepts meant. They simply did not share the concepts we do for LGBTQ people.

That left Romans 1. One of the little personal ways Papa Chuck told us to study the Bible was to say, "Any place there is a 'therefore' go back and look for the 'wherefore.'" He meant that when a passage from the Bible starts with, "Therefore" such and such happened; the indication was that there was a reason for it. In the first chapter of Romans the "wherefore" or the reason is that they knew God, but did not honor God or give thanks to God, and thinking themselves wise they became fools, and they began to build and worship idols in the shapes of other humans or animals, birds or reptiles. *Therefore*, or *because* of that, God gave them over to consuming lusts and so on. Then they became evil, deceitful, haters of God.

None of this described me. Over the years of hate mail, I have had a few people tell me that I am a "hater of God," or an "idol worshiper." Some said that I loved Winky more than God, which I found kind of silly. I mean, if I love another person more than I love God, surely the answer is not to love the person less, but to love God more. And, I rely on the One who does not look on the outward things but looks on the heart. Certainly, it did not read to me loving someone of the same sex was the central theme there.

Think about it. What if it said the same thing only said it about heterosexual behavior? If someone worshipped idols and God gave them over to insatiable lusts for sex with the opposite sex and they became boastful, greedy haters of God, would it ever occur to someone heterosexuality was wrong? Or would one think it was worship of idols and consuming lusts that were wrong?

In any case, as with a lot of things in Scripture, I did not want to debate it. I wanted to do what Jesus taught us. And for all of scripture we are to try to see the spirit or the meaning of what was being said. That was why Jesus said so many times, "You have heard it said......, But I say to you..." Then Jesus would explain the spirit or true meaning of a rule or law. He said we nitpick and are careful to "tithe" one out of every ten dill seeds but we let the widow next door starve - that sort of thing. I trusted the Holy Spirit would lead me into all truth.

It wasn't until sometime in 1983 someone told me that there was a "gay church." I thought it had to be some sort of joke or a show - all to make fun of organized religion. The last thing I expected was it would be a genuine, worshipping fellowship of Christians.

Finally, Winky and I selected a weekend when Russ was watching the kids, to go to the Metropolitan Community Church (MCC) in Costa Mesa. It was called Ocean of Life at the time. I was just shattered and amazed when I walked in the door to learn there were so many other people who were going through what I was going through and studying what I was studying. I felt at home. There were people who had graduated from Bob Jones University - an ultra-conservative school in South Carolina - who were gay and had written positive books on the subject. This church had Fuller Seminary grads who had written positively about gay and lesbian Christians as well. This church had intense, purposeful Bible studies on the subject of homosexuality as well as on other topics. They sang my favorite hymns and they preached from the Bible.

I sat there and sobbed through the service. As communion was served, people went to the front and church leaders prayed a short prayer over each person. As Winky and I made our way to the door after taking communion together for the first time, a woman who turned out to be the Pastor's spouse, said in a heavy Southern drawl, "Honey, these women love Jesus," and I burst into tears again.

We didn't go back the next weekend as I wasn't ready to bring my children but we planned to return two weeks later. The Saturday evening before we returned to MCC, Winky and I called a resort where we had reservations for a vacation later in the summer at a mountain lodge. It was a place that catered to the gay and lesbian community. Winky and I could stay in one room and not feel self-conscious. The person who answered said the resort was under new management.

I replied, somewhat hesitantly, "Oh … do you still cater to the gay and lesbian community?" She responded, "Well, personally my husband and I are Christians but it's none of our business what you do in your room." Her tone should have left no doubt she felt strongly that "Christian" and "gay" did not belong together in the same sentence. But I responded cheerfully, "Oh, praise God. We're Christians too!" The woman absolutely flipped out. She screamed at me I could not be a Christian and be gay. This was the first time someone had been so openly disdainful and hateful to me. Others had said even more hurtful things, but no one had stated it this clearly – you're gay and you'll burn in hell. Period.

I thought, "Wow … OK, let's cancel this reservation."

The next morning, we walked back into the MCC church, and I was still stinging from the woman on the phone the night before. I whispered a quick prayer as I walked in, asking the Lord to let me know if we were… OK with each other. It was a simple, "Father, let me know that I'm on the right track here." Just then a woman named Kathy bounced up to me and announced, "You missed the Gay Pride celebrations last weekend!"

I had no idea what she was talking about. Then she added, "But I got this for you." Before I could even read the button, she pinned it on my blouse. I looked and it said, "Born Again Lesbian." I thought, *"Thank you, Lord."* Her thoughtfulness was a sweet simple answer to prayer. I asked Jesus if I was on the right track with Him and seconds later someone pinned a Born Again Lesbian pin on me. But that meant something else too. *If someone had made these pins there were more of us!*

# 37
# MCC

Winky and I became more active at MCC Ocean of Life. This was our first time back in church for a few years. After over 4 years of not singing, I was tentatively singing at church from time to time. It was a new experience for me to sing alone and at first I had the same stage fright I'd had when I was 15 and 16 years old changing to songs on which my sister sang the main parts, but now I had to sing on alone. We were also able to find other gay Christians and study the Bible with them.

I knew a man named Troy Perry had started the MCC denomination. Someone at church told me I should go hear him preach the next Friday night at a church in West Hollywood. Winky and I went and found seats near the back. About halfway through the service we saw someone run up on the platform and whisper in Troy Perry's ear. His head went up and his eyes scanned the crowd in my direction.

Keep in mind here that we were in Southern California near what historians have called "ground zero of the Jesus Movement explosion." My own singing, touring and songwriting were much more recent history. Winky had seen the same look many times. Usually it meant I had been recognized in public, at the movies or in a restaurant. Winky had a custom of instantly walking along as though she never knew me. It was just a habit of closeted living.

This time Troy's face lit up and he stood and said "there is someone special here tonight. Marsha, I wonder if you would come up and sing for us?" I tried to demure, saying I didn't really do that anymore. I've told many people over the ensuing years, that arguing with Troy Perry is almost always a hopeless enterprise, especially if he has the microphone, so I'll just skip to the end and say, I sang. And I actually enjoyed ministering once more.

After the service, Troy caught me again. "Marsha," he said in his booming southern drawl, "we have what's called a General Conference coming up and the theme is 'Free to Be.' I'd like you to write a theme song for it." I started to object, but Troy would not hear my excuses. Then he started speaking my language. He quoted Scripture. The fact he expected me to finish his thoughts, and to know the references, created an instant bond for me, too. He was not taking 'no' for an answer.

"Marsha Stevens! How do you know it wasn't for such a time as this you came into the Kingdom? You cannot remain silent. The gifts and calling of God are what? Say it with me: WITHOUT repentance."

He took a breath to continue but I had stopped with his first reference. He was quoting from the book of Esther. Esther, the queen of Persia, was challenged by her cousin, Mordecai, whom the Scriptures say had adopted her to be his own daughter. If she put her own life on the line, there was a chance she could save the Jewish people but she had to "come out" to the king as a Jew. What Mordecai said to her was, "If you remain silent at this time, deliverance will arise to the Jews from another place; but you and your father's house will be destroyed; and who knows whether you have come to the kingdom for such a time as this?"

I froze even as Troy went on. Could that even be true? Was it possible I was not only tolerable to God as a lesbian; not only loved in spite of myself; but this was the plan for my life all along? Were there that many other gay Christians praying to die in an accident rather than come out? Were there really others staying up late nights trying to see for themselves what the Scripture said, afraid to take anyone else with them to see a movie about Jesus? Was Jesus really giving me the opportunity to speak up for "my people," no matter what the cost? Some lingering fear, not of hell or brimstone, but of disappointing God, died its last death in me.

I went home and began work on the lyrics to reflect the theme of Free to Be. I was nervous. I did not hear the melody in my mind as I wrote and I had no co-writers any more. How I missed the collaboration with Pete! When I heard that there was an MCC music conference coming up in San Diego, I thought we could at least go and see what kind of music MCC churches were accustomed to sharing.

It turned out the music was incredible. There was a gospel quartet that had just won the Johnny Mann Singers Award. Another wonderful piano player songwriter shared his talents. That was huge to me to see so many talented and gifted gay musicians and singers. I had somehow thought "we" would be the dregs and outcasts and here were these fabulously talented and dedicated music ministers.

During the conference I looked around and noticed my high school choir director. He was the one who had insisted I copyright my first song. He was sitting just a row behind me. I had the hardest time calling him by his first name, Ken, so I called out, "Mr. Caton!" He was a bit more astonished to find me there but we spent some time catching up. He offered to take a look at my lyrics and see if he could write the music to *Free to Be*.

The MCC General Conference was held in Sacramento, California in 1985. Winky and I drove up with Ken. I had no idea that I was a bit of a party crasher. Danny Ray was the music director for the conference and had already spent careful months planning out all the music. Here I show up with sheet music and say, "Umm, hi. Troy Perry asked me to write a song. Can I sing it?" But Danny was perfectly gracious and said there was a talent show Thursday afternoon and I could sing two songs there.

I was more out of touch than I realized. I sang *"Free to Be" and "For Those Tears I Died"* and it brought the house down. I understood it was not because I was some great singer. They already had many really talented singers and musicians. Somehow I was an emissary from the past, building a bridge I didn't even know was missing.

Hundreds of people there had stories about my music, especially about *"For Those Tears."* Some told me it was playing the night they gave their hearts to the Lord at 14 years old; it was sung at their Grandma's funeral; or it was the first song they learned on guitar.

And I was one of them.

Somehow we all met in that place of realization I did not have to 'come out' to God. Jesus was not up in heaven saying, "Oh no! Give her these nice songs and look what she turned out to be. Who knew?" Jesus was saying, "Look. I've known you and loved you all along." It was a new awakening in my spirit and I was ready to accept, "For such a time as this!"

Winky was on her own journey of discovery. She sought out counseling to deal with some of the issues of her own past. Then, one day, she received a letter from a man who had severely abused her. He said that he had "met the Lord and become a Christian. This both infuriated and frightened Winky. She had been living for the day when he would receive the just punishment in hell for all he had done. The idea weighed heavily on her soul he would receive God's forgiveness and escape his punishment – and she would have to share heaven with him.

After struggling with these thoughts for some time, I traveled with her to Maine, where her abuser was living in a rest home. When we finally went to see the man, she had no idea what she would say to him since there was no way for him to make things right. When he saw her, he began to cry.

She said, "You know, don't act like you're the wounded person here. I can't believe I'm here talking to you. I guess the main thing I want to know is ... how dare you get all forgiven by God and never even apologize to me?" Her tone was typical Winky – straight to the heart, and completely understandable.

He responded, "I could never apologize to you because what I did to you is beyond what any human being should ever forgive. If I said that to you, it would imply the ball was in your court to forgive me. I don't think you should forgive me. It was terrible. No one should forgive that." He paused. "When I first became a Christian, for almost two years I had nightmares every night of being raped, being held down, being a captive. Even though I would wake up in a sweat, crying and shaking, I thought, 'Well, I deserve that.' I couldn't even pray for God to take it away because I felt I had it coming. Then one night after a dream like that, I just felt Jesus' presence telling me, 'You don't get it. That's what I took on myself on the cross. I bore your sins. You don't have to hold on to all that horror anymore.' Finally, I was able to let it go. I stopped having the nightmares. But I would never impose that on you to expect you to forgive me."

No one could have scripted that exchange. It was what Winky needed to hear even though she didn't know it. It was such a huge thing for her to ever think she would be able to share heaven with the man who had done all those things to her. That was an enormously healing trip for both of us. I was thankful I got to be a part of it. The experience modeled for us how thoroughly God can forgive someone, how much God can change a human heart.

# 38
# EVANGELICALS CONCERNED
# AND DR. BLAIR

Following my first appearance at the Metropolitan Community Churches General Conference in 1985, I received a handwritten letter from Dr. Ralph Blair, the executive director of the LGBTQ affirming organization called "Evangelicals Concerned." He invited me to be the keynote speaker at his organization's next regional conference in 1986.

Dr. Blair, a gay New York psychotherapist, had felt led to start this group back in 1975. Evangelicals Concerned (EC) was not a new church. It had begun as several Bible studies and support groups to help gay Christians come out in their own churches. Dr. Blair's letter stated he had heard about my performance at the MCC meeting and had all my albums. He asked if I would consider delivering the keynote address for the EC West Coast conference.

My first thought was only this: *"Oh, my, gosh, someone in New York knows I'm gay!"*

Apparently singing at the General Conference had unleashed the floodgates. It was both good and bad. I started getting hate mail from people who had torn my song from their hymnals so they could send the pages back to me with words of condemnation along with assurances I would spend my afterlife in hell.

Someone called me at home to say they had seen my name aligned with people who were known to be gay. If I didn't "confess" it to him, he would call my family. More than one person called to tell me to take the "Jesus is Lord" sign off my front door. Hmm. They knew where my front door was.

211

One man called me late at night (and this was in California, so there was no time-change mix up). He said he had a private jet. He would send a car to pick me up, take me to the airport, and fly me to a place where I could be deprogrammed from "THE homosexual lifestyle."

I actually gave this guy points for having a plan rather than just a message of doom. The idea of a "lifestyle" seemed very foreign to me. My "lifestyle" was just getting back to normal for me. It meant working, raising my kids, participating in church, reading the Bible, and writing songs to minister and bring the message of Jesus Christ to all God's children.

Someone from Calvary Chapel asked me to come speak to their father who, they said, was very clear at elucidating exactly why homosexuality was wrong. I decided to hear him out. This was a very interesting discussion since this man was the first conservative Christian who wanted to speak cogently to me. He first said heterosexuality was natural since it had the potential to produce offspring. He pointed out, incorrectly, I might add, there is no homosexuality in the animal realm. I told him it didn't make any real sense to me to judge my behavior by what's natural or done in the animal kingdom. That would mean, presumably, marriage would never exist, indiscriminate sexual encounters would be the norm – whoever was around when a human being had an impulse would be a good partner, as long as they were of the opposite sex. I knew he didn't believe that to be the case. But that's what happens in the animal kingdom.

Then he tried to explain the obvious (to him anyway) problems of male homosexuals by saying anything that damaged the body of another person was inherently ungodly. I did appreciate his candor and his willingness to speak frankly and rationally with me but he had forgotten the "inherent" damage to a woman's body when her hymen is torn. Still, it was a difficult topic and I respected him for taking time to talk to me.

While all of this was happening in my life, I reread the letter from Dr.

Blair several times to see whether his interest in me was sincere. I called around to some friends to see what they knew about this organization. Many had heard of it, and their impressions were positive, so I agreed to go. Ken Caton and I wrote another song for the occasion, as well. But I was so nervous! It was one thing to sing for the Metropolitan Community churches, where just about everyone was gay, but I wasn't certain about this new audience. I felt disconnected from my comfortable surroundings.

It took a while for me to understand Dr. Blair's dry sense of humor and thoughtful discussion about all of Scripture. After that encounter, we became really good friends. I found that with Evangelicals Concerned, there was a deeply rooted theological base with a greater level of accountability for its members.

On the other hand, I thought of MCC as a "gateway" for gay Christians to reconnect with their Christian roots. For example, if someone went out on a date on Saturday night he could bring the boyfriend along to church on Sunday morning. This was a nice and tolerant aspect of the MCC experience but, to my thinking, it wasn't really the best way to witness!

Still at MCC you really only had to walk in to be "out." There are so many people who finally just step in the door of an MCC and know they're home. They don't have to worry about if they'll be accepted or included or what the pastor will think when he finds out. They don't have to guess about whether the church that says, like almost every church does, they are "open" to all, actually includes the LGBTQ community. In fact, they'd probably have to "come out" in an MCC if they were straight.

I began to speak with Dr. Blair, not as a therapist but as a friend. It was good to study Scripture with him. I found it was difficult at times to have scripturally based conversations in the MCC. There was a lot of woundedness in the lives of so many. I began to understand when I thought we were going to have a lively conversation and I *said*, "Oh, I disagree with you. What about…." (some other Scripture), what the other person actually *heard* was, "You're going to hell." I longed for honest conversation that was spiritually challenging without being viewed as judgmental. I backed off those types of discussions in MCC.

My connections with Evangelicals Concerned expanded. I was able to get time off from my work as an RN and I sang next at the Midwest conference of EC in Green Bay, Wisconsin where I had my most adventurous EC experience. When I got to the airport in Green Bay I discovered the people assigned to pick me up had left after they were told no more flights were coming from my location. I had not been smart enough to bring onsite information with me. I knew everyone's home or business phone, but not even the NAME of the retreat center I needed to get to.

I tried to call Ralph but only got his office answering service who said they could only reach him in an emergency. I was stumped at what to do next. Suddenly I conceived a devious plan. Ralph Blair was Dr. Blair. I called his service again and said, "Does Dr. Blair have someone on call for him while he is out of town?" "He does not", they said. "Well, I have an emergency", I explained. "I have a patient of his, named Marsha Stevens, who I think is… suicidal. I need him to call her right away!"

Don't everybody kill me at once for lying. Ralph got the emergency call at the retreat center and knew immediately what was going on. Within the hour someone arrived at the airport to pick me up!

A few months later I was invited to the EC conference in New York. I had all the contact numbers with me that time. I was comfortable ministering to these gay Christians. It was a place where I fit in so well. Those were wonderful experiences and just what I needed at that point in my life.

One of the things I appreciated most about Ralph was the research he had done to expose the lies of the "ex-gay" movement long before it was more widely debunked in the media. As a part of the American Psychiatric Association he was involved when the Diagnostic and Statistical Manual was revised to remove homosexuality as a diagnosable mental illness in 1973.

He interviewed ten people whose lives had been profiled in an ex-gay book and, of the ten, nine were with gay partners and the tenth cried when he called her, saying she was feeling miserable. He also worked with people who had been anti-gay until their son or daughter came out as gay. Dr. Blair has continued to advocate for the gay community as a highly respected evangelical Christian.

Many evangelicals still don't realize that gay conversion therapy was proven to be consumer fraud in a state court in New Jersey in 2015, a decision affirmed by the Supreme Court because every medical expert testified gay conversion therapy cured nobody and harmed many. And every major, decades-old ex-gay ministry from the US to Australia faded into history after the leaders admitted no Christian changed his orientation from homosexual to heterosexual (after 40 years of 'change' claims). Dr. Blair was right: you can't pray away the gay and you can't pay away the gay.

# 39
# MY KIDS' STORY

**B**oth of my kids had come to me to ask about how I loved Winky. When Johnny asked, it was the middle of a church service at MCC where Rev. Elder Nancy Wilson was preaching and used a word he didn't know. He leaned over to me, "Mom, what's a lesbian?"

*Oh dear,* I thought, *here it is. Write down the date. This is when I came out to my children.* But Johnny, sensing a long, boring, adult answer on the horizon, sighed and said quickly, "It means you're just like everyone else but your husband's a girl, right?"

Close enough.

My daughter Naomi must have been about ten when I met a remarkable woman named Sylvia Pennington. Sylvia was a straight pastor and author whose work in the Lesbian, Gay, Bisexual, and Transgender community convinced her that gays need not become straight to become Christians.

She contacted me to say she was in the process of writing a book that was going to be called, *Ex-Gays: There Are None.* She wanted to include my story in it.

Now we know that is true, but at the time I thought, "Oh dear." In the eighties, it was quite an inflammatory title and could receive a lot of publicity. I was concerned how, if I were featured in the book, it might impact negatively on Naomi, who still attended school at Calvary Chapel.

Since Naomi had been attending the Maranatha Christian Academy (we all just called it MCA) on the Calvary Chapel campus, she was learning a lot of things I didn't realize. A lot of it was pretty negative on the subject of sex in general. Since she and Winky were so close, I sort of thought she would just know by her presence that Winky was the person I loved. But Naomi had not interpreted it the way I thought she had.

Naomi remembers a day at the beach with my friend, Audrey, and her kids. She heard Audrey say something about me being gay. Naomi realized this was the bad thing they talked to her about at school and she was very concerned about whether it was true. As she thought about it, she realized her own bedroom was the largest in the house; Johnny had a tiny one since he was not there full-time and the third one was where I shared a room and a bed with Winky. She was afraid, and thought (wrongly) if she asked me I'd be upset but she finally came and sat on my bed and blurted out the question; "Mom, are you gay?"

I dropped what I was doing and came to sit with her and talk. Naomi loved Winky and liked it any time she was over. Winky had her own apartment but was over often. The hardest part for Naomi was she knew it was a secret. She was not upset with us, our love, or Winky, but she was very upset she had to keep so many secrets. She felt it was disrespectful toward Winky to pretend she didn't exist or wasn't a parent to her.

A few days later at MCA out on the field during recess she told the friend who had come over Winky and I were in love and we were gay. She told her friend not to tell anyone and she promised she wouldn't tell. Two or three days later the principal of the school called the classroom. Would they please send Naomi Stevens to the principal's office?

All the kids hooted that she was in SOO much trouble. She was wracking her mind for what she had done and couldn't come up with anything but a bunch of free-floating guilt. The principal seemed extremely uncomfortable. He stuttered and faltered and finally said another student had told her parents Naomi's Mom was gay and the parents brought it to the principal. He said he had an obligation to talk to her about it.

Naomi was mortified and really afraid I'd be mad at her for telling anyone. But she felt it was one thing to make a huge omission about our family and another thing to lie to a direct question. So she told the truth. She also felt then, and still feels, it was a question the principal should have asked the parent, not a child.

A very short time later, the school had an assembly for all the students in Naomi's grade specifically to address homosexuality and its inherent sinfulness. One of the 8th grade teachers who Naomi didn't really even know came over to her with his Bible open and sat down to talk to her about how important it was for her to be a good witness to me since I was otherwise headed for hell. She felt there was a huge moat around her and no one with whom she could be honest.

Still, when I asked Naomi what she thought about me being in Sylvia Pennington's book Ex-gays There Are None, with its inflammatory title, and she responded, "Yeah, it could get around the school." I said, "So ... I kind of need to know how you feel about it. I need to respond to this lady."

Naomi rolled her eyes and said, "So what are you going to say? No, I'm not going to tell you what Jesus has done in my life?" Ouch. Cut to the chase there. Then she told me what the principal had done. I was livid. If any Christian has a problem with me, they should come to ME! I offered to take Naomi out of MCA right then if she wanted me to but, she elected to finish that grade, then leave.

At one point, I saw another of Naomi's perspectives when she was on the phone with a boy she really liked and she asked if he could go on a family picnic with us. Of course, she couldn't date yet, but even for a family event I said, "Gosh, honey, Winky and I are both going and we want to be able to pat each other's hands and call one another honey and not be on pins and needles."
She said, "Oh, OK," and ran back to the phone to continue her conversation with this boy. A moment later she returned. "OK, he knows you're gay. Now can he come?" I asked how he responded to this information. "Mom," she sighed, "he would care if I was gay."

The only time I recall being aware of how isolated Naomi felt at all was when she was in 8th grade. She had transferred to a public school. While at Calvary she had come to assume that "public" was synonymous with "evil" since she heard those words in the context of "Christian school," versus "Public School." The first several days at the new school, she seemed so stiff and guarded. I asked if she was OK, thinking maybe she was being bullied or something. She assured me everything was fine.

On "Back to School Night" both Winky and I went to check out the situation. Naomi immediately took us to meet the principal and said, "This is my Mom and this is my other Mom and if we have a problem with that we need to talk about it now." Naomi says it was a huge relief to be able to be out as the lesbians' kid.

If anything ever convinced me of the depth of my own lesbianism it was raising straight kids. The first time Naomi came home with a crush on a camp counselor I sat right down to commiserate with her. I knew just what that was like. Every year I pined for months for the counselor from the summer before. Then Naomi said, "He signed his picture for me." It hit me: 'HE! A guy? A male camp counselor?' I had to call Audrey to see if they even existed when we were going to camp. They did, I discovered. I was just unaware they were there.

In high school, Naomi got a job at age 14. She volunteered at the AIDS Services Foundation a few hours a week. She had the supporting role in the school musical. She was an involved kid. In high school, then also in college, she served as a peer counselor. She was the kind of person whose friends sought her out for advice. She won a scholarship to study in Germany for her senior year of high school, and stayed active in our MCC church.

In her first year of college Naomi was asked to serve on a panel including people from differently structured families. Some had two moms, two dads, and single parents; some were from foster homes, adopted kids, etc. The leader was concerned Naomi might be embarrassed and told her solicitously she didn't have to speak in front of what they considered her "home room" class if that was uncomfortable for her. Naomi said, "You know, the only problem you're going to have with me is that I have the most boring, conservative family in the whole room."

After college Naomi began dating a man named Chris. I watched them over a couple years of their relationship and I loved the way he loved Naomi. I loved him, too. He and I had become close. Chris' parents had struggled with mental health issues and we sort of bonded over both having grown up in families like that. More than that, we just liked each other.

After they married, she and Chris tried for ten years to have a child. I was really proud of them that, although they wanted kids, they didn't make that the focus of their lives. Instead during that time, they continued their education, and worked with foster children and continued to work in Human Services. Chris was doing intake at a homeless shelter and Naomi was working as a counselor for troubled kids.

One year Naomi and Chris attended an MCC General Conference with me where those in ministry had a chance to share their musical gifts. It was the year Troy Perry was retiring as the head of MCC churches and Naomi sang a soulful version of "The Solid Rock". I was smiling because I knew the words she was singing came from her heart. Someone leaned over to me and said, "I can see what a proud Mom you are – Naomi really sings well!" I thought, my smile has nothing to do with how well she sings. I was smiling because she meant the words. Isn't that all you really want for your kids? To know they can stand on Christ, the solid rock?

Later in the evening Jeri Ann Harvey was having a healing service. Jeri Ann was now an elder of the MCC denomination. When I first met her we compared our histories and found decades ago she had been picketing for LGBTQ rights at a park in Houston at the same time Children of the Day was doing a concert there. After I came to MCC we got to know each other well and she became a mentor to me as I developed my ministry in the LGTBQ community.

Naomi and Chris actually did not make it a practice to go around asking for prayers to have children but they decided this healing service was a special time and they would come and ask for prayers. Rev. Delores Berry, a fellow evangelist, music minister within MCC, and dear friend, was ministering at the healing service. She laid hands on Naomi and Chris to pray for them and said, "You're acting like Sarah (Abraham's wife who waited many years for a child), and you're not her." Two weeks later Naomi and her husband had the pregnancy they had prayed for. I still tell people that Delores Berry got my daughter pregnant!

Johnny did not live with Winky and me full-time and had less interaction in our early years together but he went through some very desperate times. He got deeply involved in drugs and other illegal activity. By the time he was 12 or so he knew how to hotwire a car and survive on the street. Russ and I anguished over what to do. He was in a kind of Christian military school for a year during which time he only seemed to learn more negative behaviors. He came back from there to live with me briefly before his father and I agreed on a wilderness camp for him to attend.

Wilderness camp had the positive effect of getting him off drugs, alcohol and cigarettes, but it was also a very harsh environment. By the time he went there, Russ and I were heartbroken about how to help him. Someone told me kids die in these wilderness camps but, honestly at that point, I was more concerned about him killing someone else. I know that can sound heartless but I understood Johnny: he could survive doing something to himself – say, getting paralyzed in a car accident or a thousand other outrageous disasters. But he would not have survived causing that kind of devastation to someone else.

More than one counselor told us Johnny was a sociopath unable to care about anyone else. But both Russ and I knew that wasn't true. So we hung in there and prayed and worked together, waiting for God to do the work in Johnny. Ultimately, the first song Johnny wrote years later was very telling. It was called *"Is It I, Lord?"* I thought that he meant "Here Am I," like Isaiah in chapter 6, offering to serve God. But Johnny meant, "Is it I Lord?" from Matthew 26 or Mark 14 at the Last Supper when the disciples hear Jesus saying that one of them would betray Him, and each disciple in turn asked, "Is it I, Lord? Will I be the one who betrays you?" Hardly the words of a sociopath, and just the beginning of Johnny's path back to Christ.

# 40
# THERAPY AND CHOICES

Winky and I struggled to find counseling and a way to heal together. We had ongoing problems in our relationship, as well as each of us having our difficult pasts.

Over time, I did learn to deal with my father's abuse. I realize there were other things about my father that were not part of his illness. I'm sure he did not see himself first as a predator and there was more to him. He was outgoing and gregarious. He loved poetry. He told great stories. There could be parts of me "like him" without being part of his rage or brokenness.

For me, being able to remember the pain without actually feeling it was a huge gift of forgiveness. I wish my father no ill. I have no desire to know that God is dealing out vengeance for me. My father died. God's got him. God is handling his healing. I also realized something else. The reason I survived was knowing God had been there all along. Bright moments of reprieve or of peace in my childhood came to mind and I knew Jesus was with me even then.

Over a four-year period of time I tried to find a way to write the song that would redeem my pain. I had to use all the broken pieces in my heart to weave together the lyrics of this song, which is based on the shortest verse of the King James Bible. "Jesus wept." (John 11:35)

*Jesus Wept* – Marsha Stevens-Pino

*Wish I could sing in glowing terms of family that I had*
*My mother led the choir the preacher was my Dad.*
*But other people never saw what went on as I slept,*
*And all I know for certain is, Jesus wept.*

*Daddy was my Mama's pastor when she was just thirteen.*
*He was thirty-five and hid a rage that went unseen.*
*He said the truth would kill her Mom and so the secret kept.*
*She drank to hide the bitter lie and Jesus wept.*

CHORUS:
*Jesus wept, Jesus wept*
*Wept for little girl's lost childhoods and grown up men's regrets,*
*Wept for Mommy's unbelieving and screams the church forgets,*
*But long into the deepest night there was a vigil kept.*
*Jesus saw and Jesus knew and Jesus wept.*

*They say the Bible's shortest verse is made of these two words*
*(Jesus wept)*
*It isn't Jesus saves, or Jesus heals or Jesus heard,*
*In tells me in this fallen world not all goes as God planned.*
*It helps my broken heart to know Christ understands.*

*So when at last I met You, God, I recognized Your face.*
*You were the one who hid my childhood in a strong embrace.*
*That spark that would not die was You, that strength to finally grieve,*
*The faithfulness to feel the pain, yet still believe...*

During those healing months, Winky and I both had times we felt betrayed by one another for various reasons. When we talked over the mistakes we'd made we decided a couple of things. First, we would each pick just one person to tell "our side of the story" to, and only share limited information with anyone else. We each chose a pastor to talk with. Second, we would attend different churches so each of us had space to heal. We agreed we would try always to be loving and gentle to one another but we would separate.

We both kept our word about this and Winky and I did remain close friends. She had another partner and she was happy for me when I met Cindy, the woman I would marry in 2003. We kept in touch and sent one another cards on special occasions. Winky also stayed close with my kids, especially with Naomi who really had grown up with her as closer than a stepmother.

Winky and Cindy never got to meet. Winky died from health complications of sleep hypoxia less than two weeks prior to the attacks on the World Trade Center and the Pentagon on September 11, 2001. Just before she passed away, she apparently mailed me a card, but it did not arrive until later, when mail services resumed after 9/11.

On the front of the card it said, "We're such good friends..." There was a picture of two angels in a clothing store. The caption inside said, "That I bet even our guardian angels shop together!" Under the inside picture of the angels was the comment, "Oh, those wings are just you!"

It was so like Winky to have found a way to say good-bye.

# 41
# GRIEVING

I was on a short singing trip when I got a heartbreaking phone call. My beloved brother, Charles, had died from an overdose. It was Charles who had stood by me as I grew up doing his best to protect me from my Dad whenever he could. He helped me believe I was pretty (or at least, not homely) and I could do well in school. He also tolerated my incessant lying as a teen. He could usually tell when I was lying and we developed a secret code so, when he deemed it necessary, he would look me in the eye and say, "Really?"

Lying was second nature to me as a young teen and when he said, "Really?" I owned up to whatever deceit I was offering him. Charles never judged me or gave me a reason to doubt his love for me. In my young life, he was the one person I could always turn to when I needed an empathetic ear. Now, he was gone.

When I returned from the singing trip, I found the rest of the family was upset with Charles. Whether it was because of his drug addiction or his many experiences at rehabilitation centers, no one had been willing to schedule a memorial service for Charles.

My pastor, Nancy Wilson, held a service for Charles at the MCC in Los Angeles. I was touched by the number of people outside of my family who attended the service and expressed their concern for me. No one in my family would attend but the service ministered grace and a time of closure to me and I was so grateful to my church family.

About this time, my nephew Robb (my half-sister Kay's oldest son) got in touch with me and we went to have lunch with him halfway between Orange County where we lived and San Diego where he still resides. We talked for hours about family and the loss of his mother and his Uncle Charles. Robb and I see each other rarely but he has become a rock in my life; another one of those people on whose doorstep I could always show up and be welcomed. Besides being gay and Christian, he is the family historian. He just has a gift for remembering who was born when, whom they married, where they lived or moved. We've talked long hours about family; who surprised us, disappointed us, came through for us, gave us another chance.

When Winky and I separated, I had started to regularly attend the church Nancy Wilson pastored, the MCC in Los Angeles. I loved Nancy and it was a great church community. My family life, however, was about to take another big hit.

My stepfather, or "Grampy Bill," as my kids called him, phoned to say he had gone to the doctor with a bad cough. Within days the tests came back and he learned that he had inoperable lung cancer. Bill had been a great stability in our family. My children grew up with a grandfather who was kind and attentive. Even in areas where he had strong beliefs, he would not press his beliefs on others, but love them just the same.

For instance, I once heard someone ask him what he thought about women's rights and "freedom of choice" about pregnancies. He thought a long time and said, "Well, there are some things I believe are right and some things I believe are wrong, but if you're talking about laws and legislation, I don't see why they don't just have women vote on all that."

Now, all of our attention focused on him one last time. After several weeks of intense chemotherapy his doctor saw some improvement but the chemo had rendered his immune system inert. He soon developed the same kind of pneumonia AIDS patients sometimes get because their immune systems no longer function. He called each member of our family and requested some time together before his death. Of course I went to see him.

A short time later he became very sick and my Mom took him to the hospital. Our family gathered at the hospital to say our goodbyes. We held hands around his bed and sang his favorite hymns while they disconnected him from the respirator. We kept singing for about forty-five minutes until he passed away.

We later learned that he had gone to great lengths to make things as easy as possible for my Mom. He had prepared life insurance documents for her signature, even addressing and stamping the envelopes for her. He did the same for stock shares and annuities, as well. She only had to fill in the date that he passed away and include a death certificate. I was so grateful that Dad was the only grandpa my kids ever knew. I thought my Mom was blessed to have such a sweet man in her life the second time around.

In addition to my brother Charles, I had now lost a second important man in my life. The grief group I attended at my church took on even more significance.

My sister, Wendy, and I began to take turns going to see Mommy and helping her as best we could. Mommy and I (everyone I knew called her "Mommy") had a tradition of going to the Los Angeles County Fair each year and it was Fair time again so we went together. The next day her sister, my Aunt Polly, came to stay with her for a day or two but she had driven home to feed her cats. My mother was left alone and she called my sister Wendy. Mommy seemed incoherent.

With all the times Wendy and I had taken care of our mother when she was drunk, it would have been natural for Wendy to think that Mommy was drinking again when her speech was jumbled.
Wendy, though, recognized that Mom's slurring of words did not sound like drunken speech. Mom's speaking sounded more like our father's speech had sounded after his stroke. Wendy called some neighbors of Mom's and asked them to call 9-1-1.

I was completely unaware of all this. My phone rang that evening and it was Mom's pastor. I thought he had forgotten meeting me before Dad's funeral as he spoke very formally. "Hello. This is the pastor of the LaVerne Christian Church. I am sorry to have to inform you that your mother passed away tonight." I thought he must be talking about my Dad's death just three weeks prior. But of course, he was not.

I had half-expected that she would die all those times I had aided my Mother when she was drunk. But that was before she had gotten her life straightened out; before she had met my stepfather; before she was happy.

Now the news hit me hard. First it was my brother. Then nine months later, my step-dad. Now only three weeks more and Mommy was gone. Wendy and I spent hours going through the house we had grown up in. I had decided to use my portion of the proceeds to purchase a new guitar. My Mom had often been the first one I called to share a new song. I knew when I used the new guitar I would feel her there sharing it with me still.

# 42
# FOR SUCH A TIME AS THIS

Around this time there was a growing conviction I needed to commit more time to ministering to and with the Christian gay community. This was and is my calling in life and, no matter what else was going on, Jesus was my anchor and I knew so many people living without Him. I would often joke I wrote Contemporary Christian Music for the gay and Lesbian community. It's a narrow field, but it's wide open! In 1986, as part of that calling, I formed a Music Ministry called Born Again Lesbian Music (BALM) and began to publish my own music through that medium.

In March 1993 my beloved Christian mentor, Lonnie Frisbee, died from AIDS-related complications. He had never reconciled his faith with his orientation. At his funeral Calvary Chapel's Chuck Smith eulogized Frisbee as a Samson-like figure from the Bible. It seemed that Chuck felt God had done many great works through Lonnie but, in the end, he was an unfortunate victim of the bad "choice" he made. This seemed so unfair to me; to rewrite the story of this amazing believer at the center of the Jesus Movement; someone who hid his sexual orientation for this very reason, because he knew poorly informed fellow Christians would define his life by it.

The need for Christian ministry to the LGBTQ community had never seemed clearer so I took a temporary leave from nursing and went on a concert tour with a gay southern gospel group called "Heartsong." This was a unique experience for me as I had never booked appearances in gay bars or clubs. It just wasn't where I thought I fit in. However, Heartsong had several such engagements where I sang as well.

At one bar the management asked me to sing only upbeat songs. They feared serious songs would negatively affect the atmosphere. I agreed to consider the environment but I also felt I should not agree to limit myself to songs any venue deemed acceptable. I am who I am and that means I will always seek to present Jesus as my Savior and Lord in my music. On this occasion I sang *"For Those Tears I Died"* at the end of my set.

People, many in tears, poured across the bar toward me in response to the song. One man in particular touched my heart when he said, "I used to be born again." I felt horrible to hear this. How tragic someone who longs for a relationship with the Lord would feel aborted from the Gospel.

I said, "You can't 'used to be' born. The God calling you then is calling you now." We cried and prayed together. I assured him God never stops loving us no matter what. He stayed in touch and wrote me several times after that about the changes God made in his life.

I began to understand my gift really is not singing or even songwriting. It's faith. I started to say God has reminded me over and over I'm loved, but that's not really right. I've never doubted or forgotten it. It's like a constant whisper in my ear. I've been wrong, impatient, lacking in understanding, and unfaithful, but as Michael W. Smith says, I have never been unloved. From my very first encounter with Jesus in 1969 I knew that there was a part of me that was permanently safe. In my deepest heart, I know God is with me in every situation.

Even when I open hate mail or hear "You'll rot in hell!" or "Unfortunately, you are a hater of God," or "you should have a millstone tied around your neck and be cast into the sea!" I am not shaken. I have that voice in my ear, a hand on my shoulder and a confidence that my relationship with God will always be secure. I don't mean to imply I had anything to do with that gift. I didn't earn it or do something to deserve it. I fall, fail, doubt, and act with impatience or intolerance. But while some people have gifts of preaching, teaching or prophesying, I have faith.

There were times I had to be reminded of what I was supposed to be doing with this faith, though. While in Nashville recording a new compilation of songs I had written I went to Christ Church on a Sunday morning. It's an enormous church and they have a wonderful choir. They are often asked to sing backup at awards programs or in country music venues. A woman began singing a song the day I was there and thousands joined in. It felt wonderful to be a part of a community of faith that belonged so completely to God. At the same time, I felt separate. This was not a gay church. I could not fully be a part of this fellowship. A kind of melancholy settled over me. I felt lonely outside of the mainstream evangelical church. I had to admit I missed that camaraderie. I felt certain I would never again feel that power of thousands of people singing along with me.

After church I headed for the airport. On the plane I was seated next to a man who turned and greeted me. I thought, *'Oh dear, I so don't want to talk to anyone right now.'* He asked what I had been doing in Nashville. I told him I had been recording an album. He brightened visibly and asked, "Have you written any songs I might know?" I said, "Oh I doubt it." He asked, "What kind of songs do you write?" I took a breath and replied, "I write contemporary Christian music for the gay and lesbian community."

He said, "Wait, so you write Christian music for gay people?" I nodded, "Yes, I do." He continued, "I'm returning home to California. Nashville is just a stopover. I was at my son's funeral. He died of AIDS. So does that mean you think he might go to heaven?"

I thought, "*Oh my, gosh, who am I? I think of myself as an evangelist and here's this poor man practically begging me to tell him the good news. How can I abandon this ministry? Why should I care if I'm singing for thousands of people when there's not one to tell this grieving father about Christ's love?*"

My seatmate went on to say his family had had a difficult time even finding a place that would bury his son. The body had to be cremated. In that moment I realized the longing I'd had for the thousands of people singing along was nothing I would worry about again.

How could that ever enter my mind when there is this kind of hunger in the world? I'm not Samuel or Moses but I am God's person for people like the man seated next to me simply because I know God's love is so great for His rainbow children. So we talked about Jesus and His love throughout the rest of the flight. I knew I was right where I needed to be.

I had been looking to purchase a motorhome to use to travel to concerts. The idea of living in a motor home was not new to me nor was it uncomfortable. Children of the Day had traveled in such accommodations and I was used to these living conditions. The issue was giving up full-time employment and committing to such a large financial obligation. I had been working full-time as a nurse so this would be a big change. I felt ready, though.

I found an RV I thought would work. I applied for financing on a motor home and awaited the outcome. I prayed, asking God to open the door to this new thing if that was the right path for me to walk. Two days later I got a call from my human resources supervisor. The hospital I worked for was reorganizing and layoffs were imminent, including my own.

This was completely unexpected for all of us and I thought right away of one of my friends who was a new mother and how devastating this would be for her. Just before I hung up I thought about the fact this would mean I couldn't get a loan without a job. I asked my supervisor if she had been contacted by the loan company. She explained she had spoken to the bank just the previous day. However, she said she was not permitted to discuss the impending layoffs until this morning at 10 AM. So she had merely confirmed my employment status.

Two hours after this conversation, I received notice my loan was approved. I was able to purchase the motor home and it was sort of now or never. I had to decide if I was ready to begin a new phase in my life. I took it as God's intervention my nursing job ended just as my new full-time ministry began.

So a door opened and I walked through. And nothing had changed. I had Good News for hungry people all around me....

*Hannah smiled. "So that was a while ago now, right? Did you ever think you'd be in history books or be here at a conference like this one?" No I sure hadn't. It made a part of me feel pretty old but, then again, I've spent my life telling "the old, old story." That's always been my favorite verse of my favorite hymn: "I love to tell the story, for those who know it best seem hungering and thirsting to hear it, like the rest." (Katherine Hankey, circa 1866) "Do you still answer all your hate mail?" she asked. "I actually do. I answer all my mail. It's a matter of obedience to me."*

*1Peter 3:13-15 says, "Who is going to harm you if you are eager to do good? But even if you should suffer for what is right, you are blessed. Do not fear their threats; do not be frightened. But in your hearts set apart Christ as Lord. Always be prepared to give an answer to everyone who asks you to give the reason for the hope that in within you. But do this with gentleness and respect."*

*Hannah was quiet. "Someday will you tell us the rest of the story?"*
*"Sure," I said, "I'm telling it all the time."*

~~~~~~~~~~~~~~~~~~~~~~~~~~~~~~~~~~~~~~~~~~~~~~~~~~~~

There is more to this story, of course, and a lot of the time I minister now is online with those who have questions for me - or condemnation to communicate to me. This is one of my favorite correspondences:

"3/25/2008
Hello Marsha,
I just felt led to write to you and say "thank you" for writing such a beautiful, Spirit-filled song in "For Those Tears I Died", as well as for how you have handled so much rejection with grace and kindness. I know this is about 40 years late, but it is sincere nevertheless. I first heard about the harsh and hateful reaction you received when you came out several years ago. I was serving as a pastor, and a seminary intern I was working with shared some things she had learned about your situation. You may wonder what prompts me to write this now.

My wife and I have a daughter, our youngest. She came out to us last year...since then we have been trying — and not yet fully succeeding - to come to an understanding of this. As a straight evangelical Christian, I have had to do some soul-searching. Continuing to love and affirm our daughter has not been difficult, but I'm still in partial denial about her lifestyle. She lives in another state with her partner.

Also, our daughter's situation has prompted me to at least begin to rethink my personal understanding of Scripture. May I ask you a question? Do you believe that it's necessary to have full acceptance of someone's life situation in order to have a meaningful, even loving relationship? I mean, I have felt pain as I have read about some of the many times you have suffered at the hands of other Christians, and I admire how you seem to handle this. I also have no desire to add to your pain. On the other hand, my understanding of Scripture remains basically unchanged. I may not get to a place of full acceptance in this life. I do believe one thing with confidence, though, and that is that God's love and acceptance of each of us as we are is unconditional, even if we have areas of rebellion or misunderstanding in us. I also know that I have no time to focus on any specks that may be in someone else's eye while there are logs in my own. But I still wonder if a relationship can be authentic and loving even in the absence of agreement.

If you feel inclined to reply, I would appreciate it very much."

3/30/08
Dear (brother in Christ)

First of all, please forgive the tardiness of my reply. I'm usually better with emails, but I wanted to take some time to answer you. So... first of all, let me thank you for your kind words. I was actually very blessed to become a Christian and do all my early learning about Christ and the Bible in a church like Calvary which was (then) so open to all. Back then, you know, it was generally assumed that hippies couldn't be saved :-) ...So you can see that it was not a foreign experience for me to come across a roadblock in my life where others saw or understood Scripture differently than I, and stop to search for myself what the Scripture said. I don't want to debate it all with you. If you'd like to sometime, I'll tell you what I believe about what the Scripture teaches about homosexuality. But I did come to believe it taught something very different than what I'd been told.

The bottom line, though, is that I related to the Gentiles at Cornelius' house. I mean, here's Peter on a rooftop being told by God to do something that the Scripture clearly says NOT to do -eat these un-Kosher foods. Peter answers, of course, with the most famous oxymoron in the Bible, "No, Lord." But God does not give Peter some better interpretation of ancient Hebrew words or send Peter to the Dead Sea to find the scrolls. God just basically says, "Hey, if I have called it clean, you don't get to call it unclean." So, Peter gets it that he's supposed to go to the Gentiles...you know the story. They don't even expect to let these people in the church at all.
They're just obeying God each step of the way. SO when the Holy Spirit falls on the Gentile believers at Cornelius' house, they are stumped - how can we keep them out if God hasn't? Even in Acts 11 when Peter gets called on the carpet in Jerusalem to answer for what he's done, he does not answer with Scripture. He just tells 'em what God has done. That's actually where I aspire to be - so filled with the Holy Spirit that other believers are like the apostles in Jerusalem who were "put to silence and glorified God."

Now, having said all that, I am sorry that you are struggling so much with your daughter. First of all, love is never a losing proposition and I'm sure you know that. Whether you can disagree and still have a deep relationship is what I think you're pondering. I'll attach a song I wrote for my Mom some 25 years ago - lyrics are below - to illustrate for you that I do believe that. I'd have a couple of suggestions. In the long run, when you think there's time for it, I'd see if your daughter and her partner would be willing to set aside times to talk about where you are on the issues. I'm not sure how estranged you are right now, so it may not work. But if there's a time where each of you can say something like what you said to me - "Look I believe the

Bible teaches that this isn't the best relationship. But I love you no matter what and if I am able to love you so much, human and fallible as I am, I am positive God loves you infinitely more and whatever happens we'll work it out and love each other unconditionally." And she can say whatever she feels? Maybe "I love you too and I wish you'd be happy for me. I feel like every time you look at me you're just a little disappointed and even when I'm doing great you think 'what did I do wrong' when you see me. But if we can just let it alone for a while I'll be okay." Or something, you know? Then agree not to talk about your views on sexual orientation for a while. Or better yet, agree to revisit how you're all doing in three months or six months.

One of the hard things my Mom had was the question, "Why do you have to talk about it all the time?" I asked her to go one full week and not tell anyone that Dad was her husband. No holding hands on your walk. No pictures on the desk at work. No wedding rings. No Mr. and Mrs. Just, "This is my friend, Bill....um, yeah, he lives at my house." No couple's Weight Watcher meetings. No arm around each other in church. No square dancing (they loved that, but there was no same-sex dancing, so no dancing for them that week). She called me at the end of ONE DAY and said, "I give up!" She had no idea how many times in a day she referred to her relationship or her marriage or her marital status. "Can you come over to dinner?" "Ummm, is my friend Bill invited, too?" Ridiculous...

Okay, I've preached on long enough at you. Hope it didn't sound like a tirade. Many prayers and blessings on your relationship with your daughter. Let me know if you can hear the song - I can send it in another format if you like - and I can send more on the subject, too!

Yours in Christ's Service...still!
Marsha Stevens-Pino
(lyrics below)
*Can't We Find a Way*

*To the friends I've left behind who feel bewildered and betrayed,*
*Who will never understand the agonizing choice I've made,*
*To the dear precious loved ones who feel they've failed somehow in me,*

*I sing this song of joy and grief, "I miss you, but I'm free."*
*(Chorus)*
*Can't we find a way to make a truce of heart, if not of mind,*
*Can't we find a place of peace, where we can share the bread and wine,*
*Oh can't we find some love to salvage, can't we find some joy to share,*
*Can't we find my hand still fits in yours to say a whispered prayer,*
*Oh can't we find that just as long as God is still upon the throne*
*Our hearts are hid in Jesus and we are not our own?*

*To the friends I've left behind who feel bewildered and betrayed,*
*I love all you were to me, the memories we made,*
*I don't ask for your approval, Jesus footprints guide my way,*
*I just wish you'd let me touch you and very gently say,*
*(repeat Chorus)*
*Our hearts are hid in Jesus and we are all His own."*

His response on "4/4/2008

Dear Marsha,
I want to thank you so very much for your kind and gracious response to me. Thank you especially for sending your beautiful song that tells me that a meaningful relationship is possible even in the face of disagreements as significant as lifestyle.

I will keep your advice regarding our daughter…in mind as I communicate with her. I would like to visit her with her partner in their home (so far we've only had one brief time together in a restaurant), but to do so I would have to ignore my wife's feelings. My wife has responded with significantly more hurt and pain than I seem to feel.

(My wife) attended a seminar in Florida not long after (our daughter) came out, while she was still at the height of her pain. The seminar was given by (are you ready?) Calvary Chapel of Melbourne. A presenter stated that research shows that a primary cause of lesbianism is insufficient nurturing given to a little girl between birth and two years of age by her same-gender parent. (My wife was afraid that she was to blame.) I have not seen this research referenced anywhere else. Even if there is some study that seems to show that, what purpose does it serve to share it with people who are going to immediately start blaming themselves?

At some point I would like to discuss the relevant Scriptural references. I will reflect on your mention of Peter and the vision of unclean animals. About 15 years ago I read Mel White's book, Stranger at the Gate. I was deeply moved by his experience, but the section at the end of the book that deals with Scripture did not impress me as evidencing good exegesis. Perhaps I need to reread it. Recently I came across a video introduced by Mel White in which Fuller professor Louis Smedes discusses the oft-mentioned Romans passage. I will continue to pray and reflect on this.
Again, thank you so much for your kindness to me. You have been a blessing."

My response: "4/4/08

OH, that is so sad that your wife has been burdened with unnecessary guilt and self-doubt. What a silly debate, anyway. You could pick anything at all - people who have left-handed uncles or people who met a significant person with red hair before the age of 5 - and we'd find a way to make ourselves crazy over it. If love and prayer aren't enough, we're all lost!

I don't mind at all discussing the Scriptures. I am surprised sometimes at how we pick them apart when we are the followers of the One who kept saying that it was about the spirit, not the letter, of the law. Somehow all the, "You have heard it said that.... but I say to you..." and "in Christ there is neither Jew nor Greek, bond nor free, male nor female," and "all the law and the prophets hang on this..." just goes flyin' out the window when we approach homosexuality. (Readers of the book may want to know more about my snappy Scriptural shorthand here: references for the three quotes above are Matthew 5:21-28 where Jesus clarifies and redefines Old Testament writings; Galatians 3:28; and Matthew 22:37-40 where

Jesus says that ALL the law hangs on loving God and loving your neighbor as yourself.)

I suppose it used to happen about divorce and uppity women and slavery with the same vehemence, but today it seems to be focused on sexual orientation. It's weird how many things we casually overlook to focus there. I cannot begin to tell you how many people have told me that I can be saved, but only if I leave my homosexuality behind. Even if I believed it was a sin, I somehow never hear, "Well you can be saved, but only if you stop overeating at the potluck or smoking cigarettes or cutting people off in traffic or flirting with the woman at work or shouting at the kids." I think it's partly because people do actually sense on some level that it is an "orientation" not an "act."

So, from my humble and probably exegetically deficient perspective (hey! I think just made up that word :-) this is what I think...

In the New Testament even the words, as you know, are suspect. Certainly King James took some big leaps to translate "cowardly" as "effeminate" and then to use "effeminate" as a pejorative. Romans 1 seems to be the one that has the most plausibility as a condemnation. When I read Romans 1, though, nothing about it resonates to me   I have not rejected God or put God out of my mind, I have not abused myself or my partner (of the same sex), nor have I done what is not natural for me or worshipped the creature more than the Creator who is blessed forever.
As a result, I have not been given over to a reprobate mind or become a hater of God or any of the other outcomes spoken of there. What is hard for me is that I could look at any other Scripture with you - even ones about which we might disagree - and not be deemed disingenuous by doing so. But trying to understand a Scripture about having sex in pagan temples with prostitutes is generally regarded as me being defensive!

All of which is why I return again and again to Acts 10 and say those good ol' Gentiles at Cornelius' house sure had it right. And, I have to say, that I do not have a deal with God - you know, "let me be gay and I'll follow you." God has my permission to strike me straight any time...I do believe that the plan God has for me is the best one there is and I want to be in the middle of it, no matter what.

If you want to talk more about the Word, that's cool. In the meantime, I will be praying for all of you. ...

I just want to encourage you that doing whatever you know is right is still part of respecting your wife. I mean, we don't respect one another only by agreeing with one another, right? I really am sorry that she's in so much pain. Many prayers for wisdom in your decision-making! Marsha"

His response: "4/14/2008
Hi Marsha,
Again I thank you for your thoughtful and encouraging response. Your comments on Scripture are most thought provoking. I have been mulling them over since you sent them and I'm still processing! That's a compliment, by the way. The fact that I have no desire to respond with, "But what about this Scripture?" or some other engagement of this as an issue is kind of out-of-character for me.

I do want to ask you a question, though. You have been so kind to share openly in your words and in the beautiful songs you sent. I cried when I listened to "Can't We Find a Way?" I couldn't help applying them to my own family. And then you sent "What If They Knew?" When I listened to that I remembered all the times I felt that way as I stood in the pulpit to preach over the years.

But I said I have a question. If you are comfortable addressing it, I'd like to ask if you still wrestle with the question of homosexuality? Do you sometimes wonder if God isn't saying what you have thought He's been saying about this? In my life, I only gave the issue passing thought until I read Stranger at the Gate. Then my feelings began to change. Now I'm wrestling with my mind. Things I thought I understood I am now questioning. And I didn't really begin questioning until my daughter risked her parents' rejection by telling us the truth about herself.

Please understand that I am in no way trying to create doubt in you. I'm just wondering if you still experience doubt. And again, please ignore the question if it causes you discomfort. I don't want to ever again stand with those who practice hate in the name of the God of love.
Thanks again."

And finally my response: "4/19/08

Dear (brother in Christ) I'm sorry I take a few days to answer your questions, but I hate to hurry and give them short shrift, too. Certainly I don't see you as hateful in any way. I'm happy to "give an answer for the hope that is within me." :-)

In point of fact, I really don't ever question the homosexuality stuff anymore...In any case, that part is sort of none of my business. I'll tell you that I have a GREAT deal more anguish about my impatience, my prejudices, my haughtiness and superiority, my lack of sensitivity and failure to be kind and gentle with people. I have a lot of problems with my gluttony or food-addiction and how I fail to treat the amazing temple God has given me with health and respect as I am told to do.

Others may have more dramatic sins, but when I eat a doughnut, I am perfectly aware that I am NOT doing it simply because I enjoy the taste. I KNOW that I am doing something God does not want me to do. I do it because I am using it to deal with some other distress in my life and not trusting God with it. My whole family has died of strokes fairly young in life and I am being so ungrateful for my relatively good health when I do that. Nice for me, of course, that I have a socially acceptable addiction, but if it happened to be cocaine instead, I am afraid I would be right there, disobeying God and choosing my addiction. I just happen to look better to the world with my addiction.

And the whole patience thing? Golly, when I think of the way I drive around a clunky driver, or get all uppity with some consumer support person who doesn't understand English well enough to deal with my problem or who isn't smart enough to fix it fast enough for me - I just cringe. I don't cuss or scream, of course. My sins are far better honed and more insidious than that. I just make people feel worthless or stupid or hopeless in their jobs. I remember a poem I learned as a kid:

(by G.A. Studdert-Kennedy)
*"When Jesus came to Golgotha, they nailed him to a tree.*
*They drove great nails through hands and feet and made a Calvary.*
*They crowned him with a crown of thorns, red were his wounds and deep,*
*For men were crude and cruel then, and human life was cheap.*

*When Jesus came to Birmingham, they only passed him by,*
*They would not touch a hair of him, they simply let him die.*
*For men had grown more tender now, they would not cause him pain,*
*They only just walked down the street and left him in the rain.*
*Still Jesus cried, "Forgive them, for they know not what they do,"*
*And still it rained the bitter rain that drenched him through and through.*
*The crowds went home and left the scene without a soul to see*
*And Jesus knelt against a wall...and begged for Calvary."*

I'm an expert at those quiet cruel sins. Those are the ones that pierce my heart and send me in tears to my knees; that wake me in the night searching my heart for what I need to do to bring ALL things under the dominion of Christ in my life.

Loving Cindy? Not so much.

Hope that helps! Marsha"

~~~~~~~~~~~~~~~~~~~~~~~~~~~~~~~~~~~~~~~~~~~~~~~~~~

From the Encyclopedia of Contemporary Christian Music:
(If Larry Norman is to be called the father of Christian Rock, then

243

Marsha Stevens certainly deserves to be known as the mother of contemporary Christian music, a title that *Christian Century* and others have bestowed upon her. She was the leader of what is considered to be the world's first contemporary Christian music group, Children of the Day, and she has continued as a solo artist to produce albums of worship-oriented and edifying adult contemporary pop. As such, she remains the progenitor of what, by 2002, would become the single most popular genre in the contemporary Christian music market. Such artists as Susan Ashton, Margaret Becker, Amy Grant, Kim Hill, Twila Paris, Sandi Patty and Jaci Velasquez all sing in her shadow. Whether they know it or not, Marsha Stevens went before them to prepare the way – against odds they can scarcely imagine. A pioneer of pioneers, Stevens would be one of the only artists from the early Jesus movement to be still recording and touring full-time at the end of the millennium. And yet – she would remain virtually unknown to potential fans for her music, ostracized by an industry whose limits of ecumenicity had been tried and found wanting. The story of Marsha Stevens in many ways parallels the story of the Jesus movement itself. That revival began with spontaneous waves of spiritual renewal and impassioned piety; it ended with controlled legalism that replaced spiritual agendas with political ones. Whether the Jesus movement of the 1970's morphed into the Religious Right of the 80's or was killed by it is a matter of historical perspective. In any case, and whoever may be to blame, by the end of the 70's, the Spirit had been quenched and revival was over. Stevens, who had perhaps typified the revival better than anyone else, was caught in the transition and became one of the first victims of the new order. Whatever one may think of the issues involved, the Christian music community's rejection of Marsha Stevens remains an ugly mark on its legacy, and a prime example of its often unacknowledged sectarian character.

Born Marsha Carter, the talented performer wrote what would become Children of the Day's classic hit, "*For Those Tears I Died (Come to the Water)*" when she was just sixteen. One of the most popular songs of the Jesus movement, "*For Those Tears I Died*" is a moving testimony to God's saving grace, replete with images of baptism and liberation...the song was featured on what was destined to become the most important Christian music album of all time, Maranatha's *The Everlastin' Living Jesus Music Concert,* the record that put the Jesus movement revival into high gear, spreading its influence from Calvary Chapel in Costa Mesa throughout the country and beyond. *"For Those Tears I Died"* became one of the best-known Christian folk songs of the decade. It would be translated into numbers of languages, recorded by countless artists and, for a time, could be found in practically every evangelical songbook in the country. No one in 1969 could have predicted it would have such influence in the decade ahead – much less that, for two decades beyond the, Christian congregations would be ripping the song out of their hymnals, systematically binding up the pages and mailing them off to Stevens as a symbol of the hostility they felt toward one who continued to love Jesus and sing His praises when they thought she was no longer entitled to do so...

Stevens became the first and as of 2002 (Jennifer Knapp came later), the only major singer in the Contemporary Christian music subculture to identify herself publicly as a lesbian...*Christian Century Magazine* has said that Stevens became "conservative Christianity's worst nightmare – a Jesus-loving, Bible-believing, God-fearing lesbian Christian."

Somewhat ironically, Stevens has continued to represent "the spirit of the Jesus movement" more faithfully than anyone else from that era. In the early '70s, Christian bands often traveled the country in vans or buses, playing wherever and whenever they could in exchange for a free-will offering and a chance to give their testimonies. Likewise, Stevens spent the (past several years) in an RV doing from 120-200 concerts a year...she eschews worldly possessions, fame, fortune and all the rest for the simple opportunity of telling the old, old story of Jesus and His love.

For her part, Marsha does not betray a shred of bitterness toward any of those who have opposed her and she does not seem to resent her exclusion from the contemporary music culture. She speaks tenderly of her former colleagues and respectfully of the leaders at...churches that have dismissed or denounced her... and she has found her calling...I write and sing contemporary Christian music for the LGBTQ community. It may be a narrow field, but hey, it's wide open!"


You can read more about Marsha on her website:
www.BalmMinistries.net

# Comments:

★Rev. Dr. Nancy Wilson, author, Moderator of the Universal Fellowship of Metropolitan Community Churches UFMCC

Marsha Stevens tells the story of her encounter with the living God in the passionate days of the Jesus movement – a story that led her to trust the God who made her, and called her, ultimately, to claim her identity and mission as a Born Again Lesbian! This is a story of two movements, a world-class hymn, and the powerful intersection of grace, identity and calling. The faith that birthed "For Those Tears I Died (Come to the Water)," eventually birthed "Free to Be," and so much more. From the almost surreal accounts of founding "Children of the Day," and ministering with celebrities in the global Jesus movement concerts, to the humblest of venues, Marsha is courageously authentic. She is the "mother of contemporary Christian music," who was at the very center and then driven to the margins. A prophetic poet and lyricist, she never stops reaching out to those who are not sure they can trust God, church or themselves. Her message, is, always, "of course you can!" Of all the things that live on after us, Marsha's music may be what best captures all that we tried to be and do for our community.

*Rev. Freda Smith, clergy person who performed the first U.S. same-sex wedding conducted with a government-issued civil marriage license in Denver, Colorado for Richard Adams and Anthony Sullivan in 1975. The marriage is still listed on the Colorado Bureau of Records website.

For Those Tears I Died by Marsha Stevens-Pino is a must-read autobiography by an uniquely gifted songwriter and artist whose music and ministry has touched and changed our world.
"Music builds the Church" is an expression my congregation heard every Sunday as I introduced special music directly before I preached. I knew that nothing opened hearts and minds to a message of love,

power, and possibilities as effectively as the subtle touch of song. My church loved Marsha's music long before she entered MCC. She was a spiritual rock star in the Evangelical Christian world, a global traveler who appeared with the contemporary "greats" of the time. After she appeared at the UFMCC General Conference in 1985 and told her story, whenever she was near Sacramento our growing church insisted on her presence among us. I give Marsha credit for being a positive factor in the growth of Sacramento MCC. As a denominational leader of the Universal Fellowship of Metropolitan Community Churches I was repeatedly touched and strengthened by her musical ministry to the entire denomination. I give Marsha due credit, also, for the rapid growth of the denomination as she ministered to us at Conferences. Music does build the church. Marsha's book, For Those Tears I Died (Come to the Water), goes behind the scenes, beyond the glitter of public appearances and acclaim, to introduce us to a very deep and real survivor who by the power and grace of her faith has overcome.

"That spark that would not die was You, that strength to finally grieve,

The faithfulness to feel the pain, yet still believe..."


*Rev. Elder Troy Perry, pioneer civil rights activist, Founder of UFMCC – the largest LGBTQ organization in the world: I consider Marsha a colleague and one of my closest friends, but she is also a pioneer in her own right. One thing quickly learned by any pioneer is that there is no one there to cheer when you arrive. Marsha has forged a path for hundreds of Contemporary Christian Music artists and thousands of wounded Christians to find their way back to a personal relationship with Jesus Christ. I've ministered with her in four countries and watched her music and storytelling lighten hearts, open eyes, and spark recognition of the presence of God's Holy Spirit in people who thought they would never feel that spark again.

She wrote a song for me called Lead This Pioneer and I knew she was a kindred spirit when it said,

"I left behind the life I knew, the easy choices gone.

The warmth would lure me back, but fire leads me on."

Reading her story reminds me of the passion of those years of the Jesus Movement and the legacy that Jesus music left for us. I didn't meet Marsha until a few weeks after she came out as a lesbian Christian, but I knew of her music and recognized her the first time she walked into a church where I was preaching. I knew from that moment that the path would be smoother, the way more clear, and the truth more accessible to the LGBTQ community we were both committed to reaching. She paid the price before anybody else in the Christian music world and I will never forget it.

And I knew without any doubt, as I told her that night, that she had come into the realm of God for just such a time as this.

# About the Author

"The mother of contemporary Christian music" - Excerpt from "The Encyclopedia of Contemporary Christian Music", Sept. 2002

"She is Conservative Christianity's worst nightmare: a Jesus-loving, Bible-believing, God-fearing lesbian Christian." - Christian Century Magazine

At just 16, Marsha Carter (now Stevens-Pino) shared her newly born-again Christianity with a song that went on to become one of the most widely recognized, and translated hymns in Christian circles: "For Those Tears I Died (Come to the Water)". Some historians have said it was the first song to be called "Contemporary Christian Music."

Since those modest beginnings, Marsha has continued her journey in the world of Christian Music. She shared her music first as a member of *Children of the Day*, who are considered the first music group in the Contemporary Christian Music (CCM) genre.

When she came out as a lesbian she experienced severe animosity from those who were conservative Christians, including the Christian music industry. The hostility and behavior by Christians she had ministered to, and with whom she sometimes traveled, did not deter her Christian spirit. More than ever, Stevens-Pino passionately pursues her ministry, producing inspirational and edifying songs and performing widely as a solo artist around the United States to spread the positive Christian word of Love to all of God's creation, especially to the gay and lesbian communities.

Marsha has written and recorded dozens of albums under the label of BALM Ministries. The label stood for her commitment of being a Born Again Lesbian Musician.

Marsha is free to follow the path she has chosen and to share her uplifting testimony, without apology. Faithful to the spirit of her faith and with the full support of her spouse Cindy, Marsha lives openly, with the Jesus who invited her to Come to the Water, so many years ago.